My Year of Saying *No*

Lessons I learned about saying *No*, saying *Yes*,
and bringing some balance to my life.

By Ruth Amos
Illustrated by Caleb Amos

Copyright © 2018 Ruth Amos and Caleb Amos

ruthamos.com.au

All rights reserved.

ISBN-13: 978-0-6482913-1-2

For Moz

Foreword

January 2017. I knew that things had to change. I started the year exhausted, and in an uncertain job situation as a sessional staff member at a university, and I was ready to move on.

I had spent a bit more than a year working on my health and that was now in a good place but the exhaustion remained, something had to change. I was trying to pack too much into my life and for all the wrong reasons.

I designated 2017 as, 'The year of saying *no* to everything' and began to research what that meant. I learned many lessons and I wanted to put them all together in one place. I learned about how and when and why to say *no* to things people ask you to do, or things you put on your own to-do list because you think you should. I've learned about why we feel overwhelmed, about busy-ness and putting space into our lives, about how to decide what is important and what is not.

I've shared these lessons on my blog[1] (aquietlifeblog.wordpress.com) and this book is a collation of the blog posts with a bit of extra content coming from the lessons learned in this year and the insightful comments from my readers. I hope that this can be helpful to you as well, as we all try to live simpler, more peaceful lives.

CHAPTER ONE
Where I started

My biggest temptation when writing this book was to list all the things I was doing at the beginning of my saying *no* process so that you would recognise just how busy I was. I wanted to list my job, my home duties, the care that I was taking of various people. I want you to see that I was Super Woman, that I had it all, that I was trying to do it all, that there was good reason for my near mental breakdown, for my near burnout. I wanted to justify to you my need to say *no*. Like it was some sort of competition: I'm so much busier than you are, when I go to work I have to walk sixteen miles through the snow, barefoot, uphill both ways, and so on.

Of course, the risk was that listing all my jobs would make you say, 'Is that all? I have twice as much to get through as her. What is she whinging about? Talk about first world problems.' One of the things I have learned this year is that I don't need to justify to anyone why I have to say *no*. Each one of us is different, and our ability to cope is different, and the list of things we need to do, or not do, is also different. There really is no way to compare, and the act of comparison is detrimental to everyone. I don't need to justify anything.

I really did need to start saying *no* though.

Here's a quote from my journal at the end of 2016:

> *I am still deeply emotionally fatigued. I am having trouble making decisions or forcing myself to do things that I don't really want to do. I am feeling ready to have whole days alone right now. And yet I've booked coffees for the next three days and I need more bookings to have coffee with more people. I think it's possible that one coffee a day with someone won't wreck me. But it's hard to tell, when you are bone weary. All I want to do is sit in bed and read and write and look out at the rain.*
>
> *I'd love to write a blog post but I don't have the energy. I really want to write my novel, but no energy. I want to clean the kitchen and get groceries and do office paperwork and so on but all I really want to do is sit here in bed and write and read and sleep.*

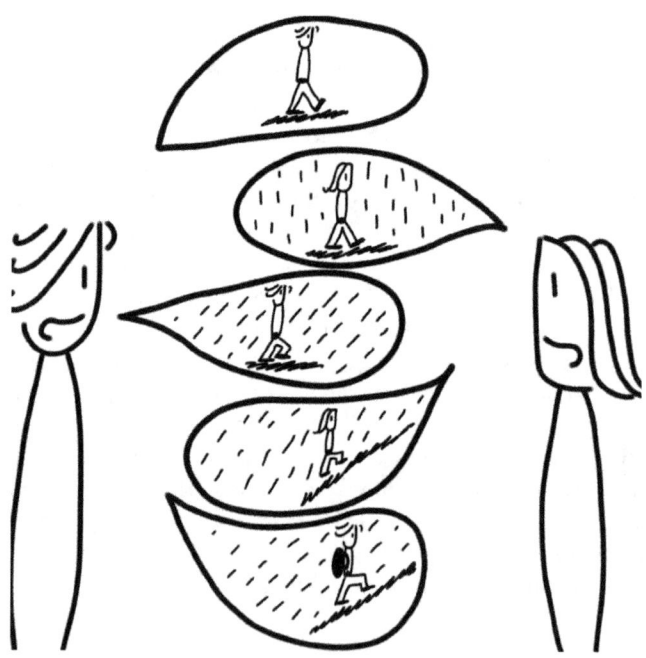

That was a journal entry in the middle of my holidays. You can hear that I needed more of a break but I wasn't allowing myself to have it. Whatever it was that I was filling my time with, it was too much for me. Things were out of whack and I knew it. I needed to learn how to say *no*.

Tiredness was something I knew very well. Bone-weariness was my old friend. I am now in my forties and I had decided at the end of 2015 that I needed to improve my health to get rid of this overwhelming tiredness. I guess that was the 2016 project.

I worked on my diet – trying to find intolerances that would mean I wasn't getting the correct nutritional value from my food. That helped a bit, I found some things that were doing me damage and I eliminated them from my diet.

I also cut down on sugar dramatically, changing my tastes so that I didn't crave the sugar in the coffee, the sugary treats, the constant sweets to get me through the day. That changed things too – the ups and downs of blood sugar were evened out and I wasn't getting the mid-afternoon crashes that I had before.

I dealt with some women's issues and sorted them and got rid of the monthly energy crisis that was being caused by them. That was great. I cannot say how much better I feel from that.

Then I went to the doctor to investigate a constantly ticking eye and severe fatigue and found that I had Graves Disease – an overactive thyroid. Treatment for that meant that my legs no longer felt like they were made of concrete; that it was actually possible to get the energy to do things again. It was incredible the change it made. If you're feeling bone weary, get your thyroid checked. It could really help.

But after all that I still felt tired.

It became embarrassing to go and see my thyroid specialist. She would say each time, 'How are you feeling?' and I would say, 'Tired. So tired.' And she would say, 'Well, your hormone levels are great so it's not the thyroid.'

And I would think, 'Damn.'

It's not that I wanted to be sick. But it was great to be able to blame the thyroid for the tiredness, to blame something out of my control, outside of myself. To be able to take a pill and feel better. But now I was taking the pill and still feeling bad, I knew that the change in my life had to come from me.

I had to simplify my life. I had to build in some free space. I had to figure out what it was I wanted to spend my limited energy on. I had to make some difficult decisions.

I had to learn how to say *no*.

How about you? Are you feeling the same way? Feeling the constant overload, the constant pull and tug to do the things you know you should do? Feeling that all the things on your list are completely overwhelming?

I hope that what is written in this book will go some way to helping you overcome these feelings. And I also suggest that you go and visit your friendly GP – it might just make a huge difference.

Of course, my other big temptation when writing this is to pretend that I know what I'm doing. That I have put all I've learned into practice and that now my life is perfect. That I don't have problems with saying *no* anymore. That my life is in balance and if you just follow my ten steps then your life will be in balance too.

I can't say I've got it right yet. I'm trying and I'm getting things more in order. But there is so much more to do, more growing to go through.

That's life though, isn't it? You keep learning until you die. I intend to keep learning and growing until I die.

So all I'm trying to do here is pass on some lessons I've learned in the past year or so in the hope that they will be helpful to someone else.

Actually, what I'm trying to do here is put into one place what I've learned from my own life and from many different places.

I tell my students (I lecture chemistry at university level) that the best way to learn something well is to teach it to someone else. (It's true, but it also helps me get through my own workload if the students do some of it themselves). So by writing all these lessons down for you, I hope to learn them more thoroughly myself.

I hope I help me. And I hope I help you.

JANUARY

I feel trapped in overload. The things I have already said yes to have filled my life and I need to deny anything else any space.

My life is so full of people – work, church, doctors appointments, friends visiting, parties, visits to friends and family. A weekend away in Adelaide is wonderful but full of people. A weekend back at home is wonderful but full of chores.

I can't even figure out how I feel each day and I write in my journal to try to get some idea. This becomes a very important discipline when Moz's grandfather passes away in almost the same week that my beloved cat has to be put down. I get so emotionally overwhelmed that I feel like I could vomit. But I keep going.

A long weekend at the end of the month gives me more energy, basically because I spend it at home catching up. And that's a good thing because February will start with Pop's funeral in Launceston – a long drive, and a long day.

CHAPTER TWO

Your personality

Let me tell you a little bit about myself. I am 'the defender' personality type by the Myers-Briggs type indicator.[2] An ISFJ. The I stands for Introvert. The rest of the letters I'm unsure about, but I really know how the introvert part affects my life.

I need alone time. A lot.

In the evenings, after work, I come home and sit on the couch, my husband and son (Moz and Caleb) hide in the study and play computer games and work, and I sit and read and watch TV and write in my journal and process the day. If this does not occur due to some evening activity then it's not a disaster, but I get tired. Especially if we are out more than two or three evenings a week.

I get my energy from being alone.

I understand that it is not only introverts who need to learn how to say *no*, but for me, the introversion is a big part of the situation. If I try to be out there with people for too long I soon fall into a fog of exhaustion. And so many good opportunities involve being with people.

I went to the funeral of a friend of mine from church. Her name was Rhonnie, she was an amazing woman who had lived a long and very full life. I listened to the many eulogies from people whose lives she had touched and I was stunned by what I heard. She had amazing extrovert super powers!

Rhonnie could invite near-complete strangers to come and stay at her place – to live with her for months at a time. While out walking her dog she could strike up conversations that led to life-long friendships. She could invite friends to come to her place and hang out, not for any reason, just to be company. She had meant so much to so many people and I would love to be like her.

But I'm not like her.

I invite people to dinner and the evening goes something like this:
Would you like a drink? Good.
Had the drink? Right, now it's time to eat main course.
Excellent, we've eaten, I'll clear away and serve dessert.
Do you want a coffee?
Great. That was successful.
Now go home.

I don't want people hanging around enjoying themselves until 2am. After about 9.30pm, however loved the guests are, they can go home. I need time alone to process the evening and I need to get it processed in time to get a few hours sleep.

At some point Moz and I decided that it was important for me to work part-time so that I could have hours at home by myself in order to pull myself together. I started working Monday to Thursday and then taking Fridays off.

If my Friday off works well, if I get a few hours in the middle of the day to myself, then on Saturdays I'm happy to go out for lunch, or to visit friends or family, or to do any other activity that requires being in the presence of another human being.

If my Friday off does not work, due to a doctors appointment, or a hair appointment, or extra work, or whatever thing I stupidly say *yes* to, then my Saturdays involve much sitting on the couch or sitting in bed downstairs by myself or general get-out-of-my-hair-ness.

I know that the need for hours alone has consequences for what I say *yes* to and what I say *no* to. I know that what I write in this book will therefore be more easily accessible for people who lean towards introversion on that spectrum. But I hope it helps you extroverts as well.

I mean, we're all feeling super-busy right? Everyone has too much on. Everyone needs to do more saying *no*.

One of the things I found really helpful in deciding what to say *no* to in life was working out what gives me life and what exhausts me. Realising that I have to say *no* in order to get those hours of alone time that I need. Maybe for Rhonnie saying *yes* to people was what gave her life. Maybe she had to say *no* to other things instead.

If you (like me) feel pushed around or tugged in every direction by all the wonderful and good options that you have for your life and your time then I hope what I write can help you to say *no* (without any guilt or condemnation) to those things that should not be on your plate, and to fill up your plate with the things that belong to you. With the good works you are created to do.

Here's another thing about me – I'm a pretty obedient person.

When my daughter Jess was younger she used to boss me around.

'Mum, I need a drink,' she'd say, as toddlers do.

'Yes, sure,' I'd groan, getting up from my extremely comfortable position on the couch or shutting down what I was working on and fulfilling her request immediately.

My husband Moz would tell me that I was supposed to be the parent, telling her what to do, and that when a three year-old tells you to jump, you shouldn't ask 'how high?' on the way up. But obedience has always been my first response to an order and it probably always will be.

I needed to learn to put a filter in between that response and the requests of others.

I listened to a podcast interview with Jocelyn K Glei. Jocelyn is the author of a book called *Unsubscribe: How to Kill Email Anxiety.*[3]

The interview was therefore (unsurprisingly) about email anxiety and how to deal with your inbox. She mentioned an interesting concept. She said that some people are 'guessers' and some are 'askers'.

Now, when askers need something, they ask for it. If they are visiting from another city and want to spend a month sleeping in your spare room, they ask. If they want someone to photograph their wedding, they ask. Implicit in the request is the confidence that you can say *no* at any time. They just throw the question to you, and expect you to say *no* if the task is too hard or not convenient at the moment.

However, guessers are not built like that. Guessers try to figure out if you are the best and most reasonable person to ask. They've tried to take everything into account, and they only ask if they think you'll say *yes*.

Both of these personality types are fine. The problem is when an asker asks something of a guesser. Then the guesser feels very guilty about saying *no* to the request and often ends up doing something they really don't want to do because they assume that it would be dreadful if they didn't. They assume that they are the only one who can fulfil the request and that all other options have been tried.

You can guess what type of person I am.

I found the idea really freeing. The idea that I may not even be expected to answer all requests with a *yes*. That the asker might be just as happy for me to say *no*.

People don't even need to ask me sometimes – I obey the call of technology without thinking.

When my phone rings I jump to answer it. Moz gets frustrated with me, especially at meal times.

'Just leave it,' he says, 'you can ring back.'

Which is quite true, but leaving a ringing phone is incredibly difficult for me.

I've even answered the phone while sitting on the toilet. But only once. Never again. Believe me, it's not a good idea.

I spent a long time trying to work out why I have this compulsion to answer every phone call. I think I've figured it out.

I only make a phone call when there is no other option. If I can text, I will text. If the conversation requires more words than are easy to text I will use messenger on my computer so that I can easily touch type. I only ring someone when I need an answer right now. Almost every phone call I make has a sense of urgency.

I need to remember that other people don't work like that. Jess, for example, prefers to call than text. She will only text when there is no other option.

People are different in the way they approach these things, and this means that I don't need to jump to answer whenever my phone rings. I need to prioritise.

I like to help people out. I like to answer their phone calls. I like to be able to solve their problems and give them a hand. But I cannot do that for every request that ends up in my email inbox. I can't spend quality time with my family if I'm talking on the phone. I can't fill up my life with everyone else's priorities and put my own priorities on the bottom of the list.

I am not expected to fulfil every single request that is put to me and neither are you. I think that most people actually expect you to decide whether what they have asked is what you want/worth your time/necessary and to make a decision accordingly.

One of my blog readers suggested that the phrase, 'Let me think about it and give you an answer tomorrow,' is very helpful. It helps us take time to listen to our feelings and to work out the best response.

Total, instant, joyful obedience is only due to God and no one else. For every other request or demand maybe it is a good idea to put some space between the request and the answer. Maybe the space is a few days, but sometimes it only needs to be half a minute, just enough time to process, prioritise, and make sure this is something that you need to do.

OK, now that you've gotten to know me a little bit, and maybe got to see how I've got myself into this mess of always saying *yes*, and always feeling tired, now let's have a look in a bit of detail at some more strategies that I've used to learn to say *no* and to bring more rest into my life.

FEBRUARY

February is a long month of physical, mental, and emotional tiredness. My head is all over the place, I need a long walk to calm myself, but I don't have time for a long walk. I feel behind at work, and behind with my writing. I berate myself for not trying harder. I ask Moz if he regrets marrying me. (He doesn't.)

I am panicking about the teaching I need to do in the new university year and the lack of time I have had to prepare, and the slightest extra stress makes me want to kill everyone. I even manage to break crockery while washing up. Everything is a big deal.

Then I take a day off and spend it alone recovering and the difference is immense. I realise I need some time each week for rest and rejuvenation, time for headspace, time to write. But I also need time to do household tasks, time to meet with people, time to go to doctors and other appointments. I only have one day a week that I am not at work. How much time off do I need, and how much should I give to others or spend on appointments, or spend on the writing?

I like the juggle of work and home, within reason. But as summer school ends and semester one approaches I am completely exhausted.

CHAPTER THREE

What is your dream life?

Life is full of possibilities.

If you read any self-help book, any blog on entrepreneurship, the back of any cornflakes packet, you will see that you have to trim down those possibilities. You cannot do everything. You cannot have it all. At least, not all at once.

And it's hard work to figure out what to say *yes* to. At least it was for me.

I tend to think that other people's ideas are better than mine, that they've thought it through more, that they know what's going on more than I do.

So when someone asks me to do something, I tend to say *yes*.

But doing what everyone else tells you to do is exhausting. You just cannot fit it all in. At some point, some decisions have to be made. And as you are the only one living your specific life with your specific burdens and challenges and your specific energy levels, you are the one who needs to make the decisions about what your life holds.

You know the analogy with the jar and the rocks, pebbles, sand, and water? I have always had trouble with that analogy. Putting sharp, angry rocks in a glass jar? What happens if you push too hard and the jar breaks? It took me a while to get past that but I saw a video[4] the other day with some ping-pong balls instead of the rocks, beads instead of the pebbles, and then sand, and then beer. And that helped.

So, just in case you are one of the three people in the western world who have not heard this analogy, this is how it works:

The jar is your life. The ping-pong balls are the big things in your life. You need to put the ping-pong balls in first: family, friends, health care, time with God. The beads are the slightly smaller but still important things: your job, house, car, looking after those. The sand is everything else. The small stuff: surfing Facebook, watching TV, that sort of stuff. The beer is just to remind you that even if your life is full, you can still have a beer with friends. (I'm not so sure about that last part, I've definitely had times where life was so full that a beer with friends would have pushed me over the edge, but maybe that's just me.)

It took me a while to understand something about this whole example, (and I may be the only one who has trouble with this) but the thing is not to just state that the important things are ping-pong balls, but to schedule time to allow these ping-pong ball things to happen. Not to just say to yourself, 'family is one of my top priorities' but to actually map out in your calendar that four nights a week you are not doing anything other than spending time with your family, that Saturday afternoon is for a family car trip, and that Sunday all the family will be going to church and eating lunch together afterwards. Schedule time for the important things first, then put in time for the less important things, and let the sand take care of itself.

OK, so this is a helpful place to start, but for me I still had difficulty with it – what are my ping-pong balls? What exactly are the important things?

I started on this saying *no* journey because of two things: I was sick and tired of always feeling sick and tired, and I had decided I wanted to make time to write. I needed to clear my schedule so that I could exercise, and make and eat healthy food, and rest, and I needed to clear my schedule so that I could follow my dream and write a book.

Now, cutting down my TV viewing and my social media time was a good start. (Notice I didn't say cutting out, just cutting down – some relaxation is important.) But it wasn't enough.

If I kept saying *yes* to party-plan parties, all the church activities, dinner with everyone, social events, work opportunities and so on, I would have neither the time nor the energy to write anything. I needed some way to divine what belonged in the 'important' category.

I made a mind-map.

You can tell how serious this is by the fact that I made a mind-map. I hate them. Lists are my thing. But I tried a few lists and they didn't quite work, so the mind-map seemed the way to go this time.

The segments of my mind-map were: Family, church, work, health, and writing. In each one of those segments I included the things I thought were important. My feeling was that if something didn't fit into one of those segments then it was sand.

Here's a new thing that I learned. In the Family section along with the cooking, washing, budgeting and shopping, I also included 'emotional energy for my family's needs' and 'Saturday adventures'. I realised that I needed to put down-time in the ping-pong ball section if I was to live the life I wanted.

The other thing for me was defining the writing as a section on its own. As its own collection of ping-pong balls.

Writing is my dream, and it is my 'thing'. It took me a long time to figure that out. Just so as you know, I'm in my mid-forties now, and I think I may have finally found the thing I love to do. I have tried many different hobbies – art, craft, exercise, maths, science, music, dance – none of them filled the gap in my life the way that writing has done. I'm hopeful now that I have found the passion of my life.

I read this amazing book called *The Art of Slow Writing* by Louise De Salvo[5] that described the lives and loves of many different authors throughout history. As I read it I found that I related to – oh, just about every category. I remember telling my friend that I wanted to write a book, but doesn't everyone? She said *no*, not everyone wants to write a book, and that maybe I should give it a try.

So I did give it a try, and I enjoyed it immensely. I enjoy the process and I enjoy the outcome.

However, in my mind my writing can be less important than any other important thing that anyone else would want me to do. You see, I don't know that I am ever going to be a successful author. In order to become a writer, I need time to practise. Time to write books that will never be seen by another human being. Time to fail. Time to learn the craft. And I have had difficulty allowing myself that time because my (maybe never seen or used by another human being) stuff just didn't seem as important as anyone else's (already out there and doing good) stuff.

I needed to change that. To change my mindset.

I've found some books really helpful to me in letting me know that it was OK to follow my dream. One is *The Best Yes* by Lysa TerKeurst.[6] She does a wonderful job of explaining that there is a job that only you can do, and that you should spend your time doing it. That it is right to say *no* to some opportunities if it stops you from doing the one thing that you should be doing.

Jon Acuff in his book *Quitter*[7] says that if you figure out what your dream is, then you will spend less time doing the things you like, and more doing the things you love. I really like the idea of filling my life with things I love, things that I am meant to do. The idea of me giving to the world a gift that only I can give, living a life with meaning and purpose.

When you have that shining orb in front of you, that reason for living, then it is easier to throw off those things that 'hinder and so easily entangle' and to 'run with perseverance the race set before you'.[8] To run my own race. To reach my own goal. To give the thing I give the best. To live my best life. For all of that, I needed to learn to say *no*. Otherwise I am like a 'wave of the sea, blown and tossed by the wind'[9] insecure, unsure, exhausted, and going nowhere.

The good book says, 'each of you should carry your own load'.[10] God has given you a load to carry. He has made us 'to do good works, which God prepared in advance for us to do'.[11] It's worth asking Him what he made you to do, thinking it through, finding out what your special shiny ping-pong ball is.

Dreams and Goals

I have learned that dreams and goals are different. A goal is a short-term, achievable stepping stone towards your dream. Your dream, according to Kristine Kathryn Rusch,[12] is a big, unachievable, shining city on a hill that you are moving towards. A dream gives you purpose. Jenny Baxter agrees. She says in her blog *Treasuring Mothers*[13] that your dream needs to be big enough that you can't achieve it on your own. You need a dream that is big enough that you are dependent on God to come through for you to make it happen. Your dream is your hope and purpose – the thing God put you on the earth to accomplish.

Have you even taken the time to dream? What is it that you would like to achieve with your life? What are you working towards? Or are you just trudging through each day doing the next thing that comes onto your list without ever looking to the future?

Having a dream really clarifies your thinking. You can work backwards from it.

Here's how it's working for me right now.

Dream: to make a living from my writing so that I can work from home writing novels and non-fiction. To get to that dream I need

1) novels and non-fiction books written by me and

2) an audience.

To get the books written I need to dedicate time to write them, time to read other books, time to research, and time to think.

To get the audience I need to build a website, write a blog, share on social media, and work with other authors.

From that point I can come up with some goals.

My major goals for 2017 were as follows:

Goal 1: Self-publish my first novel by the end of 2017

Goal 2: Write the *Saying No* blog posts

Goal 3: Clear up my schedule so that I can write more in 2018

Now as I write this I am at the end of 2017. I have not quite published my first novel but it is written and ready for copy-editing, so I have come a long way towards the goal. I have written all of the blog posts and am now collating them into a book so that I can publish a second book. And I have cut my work hours in half so that I have more time to write.

Your dream is the thing that will allow you to say *no*, and help you figure out when to say *yes*. Cherish your dream, value it, invest in it, give it your all. And make sure that you don't let all the sand eat away the time that belongs to the ping-pong ball of your dream.

So, step one towards saying *no*: figure out what you're saying *yes* to. Know your dream. Write your vision statement.

Have you found out what your shiny ping-pong ball is? Do you agree that knowing what to say *yes* to is the first step to saying *no*?

MARCH

There was another time in my life when I felt trapped in a job I wasn't coping with. My 'get out of jail free card' then was to have a baby. I took maternity leave and didn't go back. But while I loved (and still love) my kids, the stay-at-home-mum lifestyle was also difficult for an introvert like me, leaving me gasping for time alone.

I realise in March that I am looking at writing as another such 'get out of jail free card' and that, like the baby situation, writing novels is not an easy option.

I need things to change but the change cannot come without thought and care. Writing is not my saviour, I need to work out what I need in terms of type of work, time alone, budget, and all the issues, and then concoct a plan to get there. I start to wonder about building an online business. Is there any way that I can get work-life balance?

I feel like I should use all my alone time to work on my writing and get my novel finished and my new life underway, and then I realise that the word 'should' is a bad one. Definitely not to be used on something as gorgeous as writing, and not to be used for a hobby. I don't want to turn the writing into a drudgery.

CHAPTER FOUR

Should

I really should…
I don't want to but I should…

The way it works for me is this:

'I really want to sit down and do some writing. But before I do, I *should* wash the dishes, and put a load of washing on. And I really *should* ring that person, pay those bills, organise that drawer.'

By the time I get through my *shoulds* I have no energy left to write, and no idea what it was that I wanted to write about.

You'll notice that the list of *shoulds* is full of worthy and worthwhile activities. They are all good things to do. You don't usually think, 'I should lie on the couch all afternoon and watch movies.' That's a whole different type of procrastination. No, the *shoulds* are all good things that really *should* be done.

When I was trying to do everything just because I *should*, I was trying to do too much. I had things on my list that were not suited to me and that didn't fit into my schedule. It was too hard.

I had an escape when things were too hard. I have used it since my childhood. When I couldn't cope with my list of things to do, when life became overwhelming, when it was all too much, I would get sick.

I wouldn't fake being sick. I wasn't trying to please anyone except the internal taskmaster in my head. No, I would actually become sick – temperature, sore throat, runny nose, swollen glands, I need to stay in bed for a couple of days, I'm sick – kind of sick.

Let me tell you, this is not a good strategy. It is bad for your body for starters. It's a bit like jumping out of a 10th storey window just to get away from the jobs on your desk. And what if things become overwhelming because you are at the start of an exciting project – something you really want to do? You shoot yourself in the foot over and over again.

I realised in my twenties that this strategy wasn't wise and my way of coping had to change. Actually, I was being interviewed for a volunteer position at church and a wise elder asked me, 'What do you do when the wheels really fall off?'

That's when I realised what my strategy was. I replied, 'That's easy, I get sick.'

And she told me in no uncertain terms that getting sick wasn't a reasonable strategy. I needed to find another one.

I guess that was the start of my learning to say *no* journey.

I used to use the word *should* as a catch all and it was derailing all the important but non-urgent things that I really wanted to do.

In the end my husband, Moz, gave me a way to work around it.

Should became a bad word, a word that I was no longer allowed to use. I had to think about a replacement word. I had to think about why I was stressing about the task. Why it had got onto the *should* list in the first place. What was it that I actually thought about the task.

'I *should* do the washing up first,' might turn into, 'If I get the washing up done, my house will look cleaner and I'll be able to concentrate better.'

'I *should* ring that person,' might become, 'I'm feeling guilty that I haven't contacted that person in ages.'

The first task would stay on the to-do list, the second would move towards the bottom of the list.

Sometimes I would find, when I really got down to it, that the task was only on the list because I was afraid my pride would be hurt if someone worked out that I wasn't doing it. That's not a good enough reason to do anything. If the reason is 'I *should* give money to that charity because my friend who is on the board would not like me if I didn't'; or 'I have to go to that concert because everyone else is going,' that task needs to leave the list immediately.

I have found that the simple strategy of replacing the word *should* with another word or phrase has helped me to keep my to-do list shorter and to reduce the stress in my life. Maybe you can try it.

CHAPTER FIVE

Everything is worthwhile

Some things are really easy to say *no* to.

For example, I have no desire to run a marathon. And despite how wonderful my running friends say that running is, I just don't enjoy it. I love a good brisk walk in the evening but that's about as far as it goes. So I am not in any way tempted to say *yes* to fun runs, boot camps, even yoga retreats. It is very easy for me to say *no* to those.

I used to feel very bad about saying *no* to party plans. You know, those sales parties for makeup or lingerie or linen or Tupperware or cleaning products or... the list goes on and on. My good friends would ring me or send me a message telling me about this wonderful new product that they were having a party for. Actually, that's not strictly true. More often they would ring or send a message to tell me that they really didn't care about the sales, they just needed bums on seats, and they were going to provide yummy food (and in some cases, alcohol) and we could listen to the little sales spiel and then spend the rest of the time enjoying ourselves and just hanging out, and please could I come?

I would be torn. I was glad that the person thought of me. And I really understood the terror of booking a party-plan party and having no-one show up. And I wanted to be their friend and be there for them. And sometimes I even believed in the philosophy of the product that they were selling. But I really didn't want to go.

In the end, I decided that these parties were not the best use of my time. I didn't have the money to spend on them and I didn't, and don't, need more stuff. Especially stuff that I had to be talked into buying. And as much as I loved my friends and was flattered by them thinking of me, there was never time to just chat and hang out at these parties. Or at least, never time to get into the deep conversations that I like to have. Only time for small talk which I personally find exhausting.

So I am happy for others to have party-plan parties, but whenever I am asked now, the answer is always *no*. And it doesn't hurt me much to say it.

However, some things are much harder to say *no* to.

This year I found that I had to say no *to a part-time job.*

The job involved working after-hours as a tutor in a small business that tutors primary and high school students in literacy and maths. It's an excellent business, the tutors do excellent work, and it's something I totally, whole-heartedly believe in. There is also a huge need for tutors – there is always a waiting list for the business. And tutoring is something I can do. I know enough maths and science to tutor people through high school and beyond, and I could probably do high school English at a pinch.

But it was not the right thing for me to be doing.

Each week as the time came for me to begin tutoring, or as emails relating to the job came into my inbox, or as I would think about the next staff meeting, my gut would knot up, my stress levels would rise.

But when I thought about saying *no*, about quitting, I couldn't justify it. This job was only a very part-time job. I had made a commitment to keep tutoring until the end of the year, and I keep my commitments. I couldn't think of any good reason to turn the work down, except that I wanted more time for writing, more time to do the thing I knew was my thing. And that keeping on going felt all wrong.

In the end, after much conversation, my boss made it easy for me and arranged things so I could bow out gracefully. I'm very grateful to her. And I'm sure it was the right thing to do. But it wasn't easy – the job was such a worthy cause, the work was worthwhile.

There is no shortage of worthwhile things to do – worthy causes to give time to. But somehow we need to weed them out because we cannot do everything. We just can't.

Os Guinness, in his book *The Call*, expresses this wonderfully:

> In the modern world there are simply too many choices, too many people to relate to, too much to do, too much to see, too much to read, too much to catch up with and follow, too much to buy.
>
> Each choice sprouts with its own questions. Might we? Could we? Should we? Will we? Won't we? What if we had? What if we hadn't? The forest of questions leads deeper and deeper into the dark freedom, then to the ever darker anxiety of seemingly infinite possibility.
>
> At some point different to us all a cut-off switch kicks in. We are overloaded, saturated. There is too much to do and too little time to do it. But life goes on. Neither planning nor juggling can span the gap. But life goes on. At the level of our relationships alone, their sheer number, variety, and intensity becomes impossible. But life goes on. One minute we feel the vertigo of unlimited possibility and the next the frustration of superficiality. But life goes on.[14]

I'm going to explore this idea a bit more in the next few chapters. For now I want to encourage you to listen to your gut. Maybe it's time to say goodbye to a worthy activity that is just not right for you right now. Maybe you've looked at your schedule, your activities, and you've prioritised your ping-pong balls and there are very worthy things that don't fit in your jar. If that is the case, you don't need to do it all.

If you need someone's permission to drop that worthy thing, I give you permission. It's ok to say *no*.

It might be time to have that hard conversation with someone so that your life is simplified and you are more able to do the things on top of your list. My experience is that it is worth it. Hard, yes, but worth it.

Again, a beautiful quote from Os Guinness:

> Yet, as we make our contribution along the line of our gifts and callings, and others do the same, there

is both a fruitfulness and a rest in the outcome. Our gifts are used for the purpose for which they were given us. And we can rest in doing what we can without ever pretending we are more than the little people we plainly are.[14]

APRIL

April was another full month with two weddings, Easter, and a couple of trips to Launceston to do some teaching at university up there. I even got to the point where I was thinking of having a break from writing. I was done in.

But then we took a holiday. Moz and I spent a week away. Completely away. We travelled to Canberra to spend time with Jess. We spent some time just driving around by ourselves. We got away from the state of Tasmania, and I could figuratively feel the ropes snapping as the plane took off. I discovered I didn't want to take even one full day away from writing. And after the week I felt rested and rearing to go.

That feeling lasted about a week but it gave me hope that if I could get things right I could feel energetic again. I just need to do more of what I love and less of what I like. More energy-giving activities and less energy-draining activities. I need to get the balance right.

CHAPTER SIX

Time is like money

I was talking with my friend Sarah one evening about how difficult it was to say *no* to worthwhile activities and she gave me a very good piece of advice.

'Time is like money,' she said.

Now we've all heard 'Time is money' – that we need to make sure that we're using our time to make money, or that the use of our time is worth money, but that's not what she was saying. Instead, she was saying that just like we need to budget our money, we also need to budget our time.

Sarah and I had both worked through an excellent budgeting book *The Complete Cheapskate* by Mary Hunt[15] and we both approach our money management in the same way. Mary suggests giving away at least 10 per cent of your income first, and then saving at least 10 per cent for the future; then some money is put in a separate account for bills and such that you know are coming up; some is put aside to treat ourselves, and the rest is spent on food etc. (She's also very clear about getting out of debt as soon as is humanly possible.)

Sarah was saying to me that, in the same way that I know I can't give to every good cause, I can also not give my time to every worthwhile activity. I need to choose my activities, and stand by my choice.

The other day I met with my friend Megan for coffee in the city. I wasn't exactly running late but I was on a tight schedule and I was eager to spend as much time with my friend as possible.

As I turned the corner to the door of the coffee shop I was accosted by a very friendly man with a large smile and a grey beanie. (It was winter in Tasmania, it was cold.)

'Hi, nice to meet you!' he said with great enthusiasm and shook my hand and gave me his name and asked for mine.

My heart sank. I knew what was coming.

I don't like to ignore people and just walk on, especially when they give me a warm and genuine smile. It is just rude to completely blank them and I find it impossible. But sometimes I wish I could.

He was a 'charity mugger' – you know, one of those people from a non-profit organisation who is out on the street and wants, not a donation, but a commitment of 'just $40 a month, less than a coffee a day.'

What do you do in that situation? The needs in this world are huge, and if you are reading this on an ebook reader, or even in hard copy, you are probably one of the privileged few.

I love my cup of coffee a day. I would find it hard to give that up for any charity. I need to provide for my own family, pay my own bills, save for my future, and I also want to put aside some money to follow my dreams.

In one way, I would like to give every cent that I have to help a child climb out of poverty, and to help a girl escape child marriage (this is what the guy in the beanie was about), and to help a woman in a developing nation start her own business, and to boost medical research. The list goes on and on. The number of charities in Australia is doubling every decade. Pro Bono Australia counted 56,894 charities in Australia in 2016. We can't give to them all.

What are we to do?

One of my major breakthroughs when thinking about this issue was to realise that it is not my responsibility to solve every problem in the world.

I can't get my head around how many people there are in the world. There are so many people. My brain can handle the thought of ten, one hundred, one thousand people. I have at least a thousand people that I know personally. I think I can almost hold that number of faces, personalities, in my head. After that it gets fuzzy. When I'm driving home of an evening I look at all the cars and realise that each person in each car is a personality with their own dreams and trials and families, hurts and loves – I tell you it spins me out a little.

If I gave every cent of my own money to charity it wouldn't help that much. But if everyone in the developed world gave a little of their money to these charities, then we could do a lot to make the world a better place. The charity-muggers are doing an important job if they get someone who is not giving to start giving. It's a numbers game.

Let me tell you what I decided to do, not to blow my own trumpet but to maybe help you to make your own decisions.

I decided how much of my income I was going to give away. I've decided that 10 per cent of my gross income is a good way to go. I've heard of someone who lives off 10 per cent and gives away 90 per cent and, to be honest, I'd like to get there one day. But 10 per cent is a good place to start. Sometimes I give a little more out of my savings, especially when I feel like money is getting a hold on me. Giving is an excellent way to combat both greed and fear that God won't provide. But that's another story.

Once I had decided how much I was going to give, I looked at my personal values and found a number of organisations that suited my values. I'm going to give you a general idea of my giving, again not to blow my own trumpet, but so that you can hopefully use it to make your own list. I give to local and to international mission, I sponsor some children in the developing world, I give to a non-profit that supports victims of child abuse and one that supports research into cancer, and I support my local church. That's it.

I made the decision thoughtfully and prayerfully. I took my time over it. And I revisit it occasionally when I have time and brain-space. But for most of the time the decision is made.

So what did I do when the friendly man in the beanie attacked me with his very worthy cause? I said *no*.

At first, (and this turned out to be not a good idea) I tried to tell him that I gave already to five charities (yes, I forgot some) and that I had made my decision, but he was having none of it.

'That's great! You're just the kind of person I want to talk to! If you give to five, why not six?' he said.

Then I realised that I didn't need to justify to him, or to anyone, why I was not giving to his particular charity, worthy though it might be. His charity was an SEP (Someone Else's Problem). I have decided where I am going to give and that's the end of the story.

I'm sure he gets knocked back all the time and that he can deal with it. The person I have to live with is me. When I was trying to make each decision about giving on the spur of the moment I was pushed around by my own emotions, my guilt, my compassion. It was not pretty.

I'm very sure that God doesn't want us living under a cloud of condemnation all the time. In fact, he says so: 'There is therefore now no condemnation for those who are in Christ Jesus.'[16]

I don't need to feel guilty because I can't solve the world's problems. Solving the world's problems is not my job.

Giving is excellent. Giving is my job. Giving is good for me, it is good for each of us, and it is good for the world. Let's make a decision about how much we will give, and where we will give. And then give. But let's not get hung up on feeling guilty that we can't be the saviour of the world.

Now, how did I transfer this idea to my time management?

I needed to approach my time the same way that I sorted out the giving of my money. First, I figured out how much time I was prepared to give away to other people's important activities. At the time of writing this, I was working four days a week and work obviously limits the amount of time I am able to give. It cuts a massive chunk out of my time budget. (In the same way that the mortgage repayment cuts a chunk out of the money budget.)

Once I figure out how much time I have to give – it might be two activities a fortnight, or three a month – then I can say *yes* to those activities within that budget that suit my personality. But once I've used up that time, then I need to say *no*.

I can't say *yes* to all the worthwhile things that are happening, I don't have that much time in my budget. Somehow I need to make a decision that's in keeping with my personality and values and only say *yes* to a few things. Other people can make up the shortfall.

One recent activity where I had to say *no* was a Mothers Day high tea at church. It was run by our women's ministry team and I felt especially pressured (by myself, not by anyone else) to say *yes* because I had led our church service the week before and had made the announcement about the high tea. It's very hard to say, '*Do* come to this excellent activity' with any form of sincerity when you're pretty sure you won't be going yourself.

But I had had a huge week that week. I had led church, travelled to Launceston (about three hours away) and given two days of teaching at the university campus there, staying overnight to do so, and had a couple of coffee dates with various people as well as my normal workload. I knew I would be tired and I knew (as an introvert) that this high tea, while pleasant, would be exhausting. I decided not to go and removed the entry from my calendar.

I felt guilty – it was a great cause (Days for Girls[17] was being supported by this event) and I also wanted to support the amazing women who make up our women's ministry team, but my time budget was too stretched and I needed to be at home, pottering around, grocery shopping, washing things, reading books.

It turned out that one hundred and eighty women attended the high tea. They were in no way affected by me not going. I must have done a wonderful job of advertising it in the church notices! No, I'm kidding, it was nothing to do with me at all but it was a really excellent result.

It is just as stupid to blame myself for the success or failure of an activity due to my not turning up, as it would be to blame myself for a charity going under because my forty dollars a month was not going into their account. I cannot give my time to every worthwhile activity and I shouldn't be trying. I need to budget time to give regularly, and save some time (and energy) up my sleeve for special occasions that might pop up.

One of the things I love to spend my time on is coffee with people. I love one-on-one time with people, deep conversation, time for encouragement, and I also love coffee. When I am with those who don't drink coffee I allow them (grin) to drink tea or hot chocolate. The choice of hot beverage is not really important, but the time is.

I like having coffee with people because coffee generally lasts an hour. Lunch can take up more than an hour – up to two hours even, and dinner is so open-ended it scares me, but coffee is a good short time when you can have a great conversation and then get back to whatever you're doing.

If I could, I'd have a coffee with someone every day, but I've realised lately that even the one-hour coffee was putting a strain on my time budget, much the same way that buying your lunch every day can put a strain on your money budget. It all adds up.

I now limit my coffee time. I give a coffee to each of my parents every week, and I have allowed myself two more coffees each week but no more. This meant that when a friend came to me at church and asked if we could get together because she had something exciting to tell me, I had to put her off for three weeks. That felt really bad. (And it also meant that my husband found out the exciting thing before I did because it came up in a church meeting that he went to. He was very good and didn't tell me anything, and it does show that there are consequences to our actions, but that's by-the-by.) So yes, it felt bad to put her off, but it meant that when we did finally get together I was not exhausted, I was happy and eager to hear her news, and we had time to deeply share and pray about it, instead of me being rushed and needing to get back to work.

Saving money is really hard. I mean really saving – for the future. Not for a holiday or for next week or for the next time that we run out and need to buy something, but for the long term future. It's hard. I find it hard. But it's necessary. It's a good thing to do. It's good stewardship, delayed gratification, healthy and wise.

In the same way, I need to put aside time to rejuvenate myself. This is time where I have nothing booked, time just to be. Time to invest in myself and my energy so that I have energy in the future.

It is difficult to block out time for this because it doesn't have a label attached to it. It's not exercise, or doing something for someone, or cleaning the house, or working. It's rest time. Just rest.

It's easy to eat into it – 'Yes, I can do that – there's nothing booked into my calendar.' Maybe there should be 'Nothing' booked into your calendar so that you don't book anything else in. A plan to do nothing. Just to be. To read, to think, to go for a nice walk, to sleep.

Setting time aside like this is investing in your future.

Moz has found that this principle applies very well when it comes to sleep. A few years ago you would have found me heading to bed at 9:30pm and Moz would be an hour or a bit longer behind me. I have to go to bed at 9:30pm – that's when I turn into a pumpkin.

One evening a few years ago now, I came home from work, totally fruited, at about a quarter to eight, and Moz heated up my dinner and served it to me on the couch (home made pizza – yum!) and at first I didn't want to do anything but watch the box and chill out. But after a little blob time I was ready to surface and we both decided to turn off the TV and connect with each other. We talked about the day – how his work went, how mine went, interesting things that happened, interesting things people said. Then we started talking about our plans for the future, little bits and pieces, lovely conversation.

Then, in the middle of conversation, Moz looked at me, read my body language, looked at the clock and said, 'yep, it's nine-thirty. Pumpkin time.'

You see, I need a lot of sleep. About nine and a half hours a night does me beautifully. I am probably more of a morning person than an evening person but I'm not the kind of morning person who wakes at 5am refreshed and happy and ready to start the day. No-siree-bob. I am the kind of morning person who wakes very slowly and becomes an intelligent being by drinking a cup of coffee in bed. I am so incredibly privileged to have a husband who is happy to get up in the morning and bring me a cup of coffee in bed. Perhaps it's because I'm just totally useless without it.

Moz used to see me to bed once my brain stopped functioning and then he would stay up for around an hour, playing on his computer, learning things, reading articles, and then he would come to bed at ten-thirty-ish and – here's the thing – try to immediately fall asleep so that he could get his eight hours before the alarm went off in the morning.

Have you ever tried to immediately fall asleep? It adds a little stress to the scenario. Each ten-minute interval that you're not sleeping is a drama. You know that waiting ten minutes to get to sleep means you'll want to wake up ten minutes after the alarm goes off next morning and you'll therefore wake up groggy and grumpy.

When Moz was coming to bed at half past ten, woe betide me if I asked him to head back up stairs to turn the heat pump off, or to check if my phone was plugged in. He needed to fall asleep right then. Straight away.

A little while ago he decided that this was silly. Now, when pumpkin time hits and I go into the study to say goodnight, he says, 'Is it bed time?' turns off his computer, and heads to bed too. We turn off the light early and he gets his eight hours. Actually, he's worked out that he needs seven hours and fifty minutes sleep each night.

So he sleeps for seven hours and fifty minutes and wakes up naturally between 5:30 and 6am. He gets up, heads to the study, and does the things that he would have done at night. He plays computer games, reads interesting articles, and learns things. At 6:45am when the alarm goes off he makes us a cuppa and brings it down to wake me up. He's accomplished something already and he's had a restful night's sleep.

They used to say about daylight saving time that it's daft to cut one inch off the top of the blanket and put it on the bottom and say that you have a longer blanket, but it looks like that very strategy has worked for Moz. He's a happier, healthier person because he is investing his time in sleep.

I have another friend, Trish, who blocks out an entire month of every year to go on a retreat. She is a minister, and this is her way of investing in her growth and prayer life. She goes away, stops all of her commitments, and spends the month reading, writing, praying, retreating. It's saving, investing in her future.

What do I do? I make sure that I don't block up every time-window in my schedule. I make sure that I am not out in the evenings more than twice a week and that Sunday evening is kept free so that I can use it to get my head together for the week ahead. And I only work four days a week. I give myself half a day to visit with people, and half a day to be by myself, to do whatever needs doing to rejuvenate. Sometimes that means writing, sometimes reading, sometimes I lie on the couch all day and watch TV. It's time to invest in me.

I couldn't always do that, of course. When you have small children there is not much chance of time alone. Sometimes life circumstances just do not allow the space that you need. But sometimes we bring it on ourselves – the busy-ness. Is there something in your schedule that you can cut out to allow yourself some time, just to be? Is there some time-saving that you need to make for your future?

When we are feeling energetic we can budget our time so that every single moment is spent doing 'worthwhile' things. Then when we start to get tired, we can throw the budget out the window and start to 'waste time' just to feel like we are getting through. But what if the 'time wasters' were actually refreshing, renewing activities that gave us new life? Maybe if we add them to the budget in the first place we will feel less guilty and more alive. We could schedule in half an hour of Facebook or reading or TV watching and know that it was OK because we'd already thought about it.

We are responsible for using our time wisely, and giving it carefully.

I encourage you again to think about your own time budget. What can you cut out? What can you double up on? (For example, Moz and I combine our catch up time – our chatting about our day – with a walk for exercise. It makes us want to exercise and it gives us excellent communication as well.) What can you limit to once a fortnight, or once a month? What do you think about the idea of having an amount of time each week that is set aside to give away? How can you integrate clear spaces so that you are living within your time and energy limits? It is worth the energy and effort to do so.

MAY

In May we made a very clear and conscious decision that I would leave my job at the uni and be settled in my new job (whatever that was) by the beginning of 2019. I would continue until the end of my contracts (four days a week until December and then two days a week until June) and then ... something else ... But what?

I began listening to podcasts and reading books about life changes. Quitter by Jon Acuff,[7] Career Change by Joanna Penn,[18] blogs by Kristine Kathryn Rusch[12] and Dean Wesley-Smith,[19] talks from the Alpha leadership conference.[20] One blog post by Jo-Anne Berthelsen asked 'What is the invitation God is extending to you for the next part of your life?'[21]

I really started searching for the answer to that question.

I read The Pastor by Eugene Peterson[22] where talks about having work that is congruent with his personality, with who God made him to be and with the vision God had placed in his heart, and I realised that that congruence was what was missing for me in my university position. I didn't want to let my colleagues down or leave them in the lurch and I felt a bit guilty because I knew that our department was short on teaching staff, but I knew it was time for me to go.

Semester 1 finished at the end of May to my great relief. One more semester's teaching to go.

CHAPTER SEVEN

Reward yourself

I find saying *no* so incredibly hard. I don't like to let people down. I don't want to be a disappointment.

Actually, when I was a kid and my parents wanted to discipline me, all they had to say was, 'I'm so disappointed in you' and that was it. I was in my bedroom crying. True story. Up until the age of, let's say, 20 and married.

So when I started putting boundaries around my life this year I had to do two things. I had to allow myself to put the boundaries in place, and I had to reward myself for saying *no*.

First, I had to give myself permission.

I knew things were changing this year. I wanted a year with more time to do the writing I felt God was calling me to do. I wanted to feel less, less stretched. I read wonderful books like *Margin* by Richard Swenson,[23] and *The Best Yes*,[6] and I knew that in order to do what I was called to do, I would need to say *no* to some things.

To allow this to happen I designated 2017 as *The Year of Saying* NO *to Everything*.

This year I was allowed to say *no*. This year, I didn't have to feel like everything was my responsibility – it was actually my responsibility to say *no*. I didn't need to come up with reasons or excuses to back out. I didn't need to ask myself whether or not I should decline the invitation.

This was The Year of Saying NO.

One afternoon I found that it was just so helpful to have the decision made ahead of time.

You see, I was working with an amazing woman who had heaps of energy and just LOVED social occasions. Gemma is the kind of person who organises team-building activities. The kind of person who enjoys get-to-know-you games. And she was eager to build our work team into a coherent whole. One of the first things that she suggested was that we all go to an escape room together.

I don't know if you know about escape rooms. They are really popular right now. The idea is that six of you get shut in a room, locked in together, and you have to solve problems to find a way out. It's group work that you are literally locked in to.

The whole idea is comparable to my idea of hell. Really. Wouldn't like to do it even with my best friends. Can't we just go out for coffee and a chat? If you really like the puzzles we could design them ourselves.

But this was not all. She wanted to include our spouses in this experience – we hadn't even met the spouses – and then pick numbers from a hat so that we had two randomly divided groups, and then go into separate rooms, with these strangers, and race each other to get out first.

Now, like I said, these rooms are incredibly popular and they may well be your idea of a good time. I think her suggestion was a good idea. But it was not for me. And so I wanted to say *no*.

Instead of saying *no*, I said I'd check with Moz. And I did. I said, 'Hun, if going into one of these rooms is the deepest desire of your heart, then this is when we'll do it. Otherwise, let's just not go.'

So that was a *no*.

On the same day as the invitation to the escape room, Gemma also invited me to her fundraiser. Now I think this woman is incredible. She is working, raising two kids, and then in her 'spare time' she organises this HUGE fundraiser day. It's a high tea. The ladies dress up and have delicious foods and there are competitions and music and goodness knows what. It's huge. She got on the local evening news with this one.

Of course she wants everyone to go. It's important to her. It's important full stop. So she asked me, and I said *no*.

'Why not?' she said.

Oh boy. What an awful situation. Why not? What excuse can I find? Am I too busy? Not really. Did I already have something else on? No. Did I want to go? Not on your nelly.

But I had an answer. I had already decided.

Why not?

'Because this is my year of saying *no* to everything,' says I.

It was decided.

Now I know that every year can't be the year of saying *no* to everything. But I figure I need the practice. So this year is the practice year. Perhaps after I get better at setting boundaries I will just be able to say *no* and then if asked 'why not?' I will be able to think of some excuse like 'It's just not for me.' Or 'I just don't think it's right, right now.'

In *The Best Yes* Lisa TerKeurst has some great statements to give to soften your answer of *no*:

> 'While my heart wants me to say yes, the reality of my time makes this a no.'
> 'I'm sorry but I can't give it the attention it deserves.'
> 'This is one of those seasons when I must decline lovely invitations. But thank you for thinking of me.'[24]

All of these are much more gracious than my blurted answer. Maybe I need more practice.

Second, this year, I had to reward myself for saying *no*.

I've told you that I feel very bad every time I let someone down, even if I know that saying *no* in a particular situation is the absolute right thing to do.

I don't want people to be disappointed in me. Though I know in my head that I can't meet everyone's needs and expectations, I really want to.

I have thrown party-plan parties where nearly no-one has shown up. I don't want anyone to go through that. I have organised prayer meetings where week after week no-one has come along but me, and I would almost prefer to be burnt-out than have another person feel that loneliness and failure. (You might have guessed that I'm not the world's best sales-person. I am the diametric opposite to Gemma.)

I want to be able to go to all the things, meet all the needs, comfort all the people, serve on all the committees.

It's just impossible.

But what is also impossible is living with the feeling of having let so many people down.

Now that I'm getting used to saying *no*, I'm realising that I'm not necessarily doing a bad thing by letting them down. There are many instances where I would just be an unnoticed extra in the room. There are other times when maybe God wants the person to learn from something falling over (I'm pretty sure that's what was happening in my prayer group), and that if I show up and be the comforting person I will be stepping in the way of God's plan.

If I want to follow God's path for my life then I can't veer off onto something else anytime someone asks me for a favour.

So this year I decided to reward myself for saying *no*. If this was the lesson I needed to learn then I needed a shot of encouragement each time I managed to decline an activity.

Moz made me a star chart with a little path of hearts leading the princess to the castle, and I bought shiny gold stars from the local newsagent.

Every time I've said *no* to something this year I have got a gold star on my chart. I am building up to a reward at the end.

I usually check with Moz, 'Can I have a star for that one?' and he usually says *yes*. He sees the stressing and overthinking that goes on whenever I turn something down.

Here's an example:

I was invited out to dinner with my friend Dess on a Friday night. Dess is lovely, she really understands me. She said, 'If you can't come because your introverted self needs time at home, that's fine.'

My introverted self did need time at home. But the teaching at church and in some podcasts I was listening to was about how important it was to eat with people. How eating together connects us and makes us family. And Dess is very important to me. But at the same time, so was Friday night date night with Moz (we eat takeaway and watch a movie together) and I didn't know what to do.

Moz was happy with whatever I decided. Dess was happy with whatever I decided. I had to make the decision. I had to set the boundary. I wasn't so happy. I took ages to decide and in the end I sent Dess a text Friday morning saying *no*, I wouldn't come.

Did I get a star for my star chart? You betcha. And that shiny gold star made me feel better about the decision, which I'm sure now was the right one.

You may have no difficulty deciding what is right for you to do and what is not necessary. I know that some of you can't understand what my difficulty is and think I should just get over myself. (I thank you for continuing to read anyway.) But I hope that for some of you, my journey is providing a helping hand on your own journey.

And maybe it's not saying *no* that is the difficult thing for you. Maybe a star chart could be helpful in another area of your life – you could get a star for every half-hour walked, for example. Or for every time you do the dishes before going to bed.

For me, saying *no* is difficult, but the star chart helps. The reward helps. I can do a hard thing and then get some tangible appreciation of effort outlaid. It's helping me to train myself in setting boundaries and the little tool of giving myself a gold star when I succeed has made a big difference to how I feel.

Only three stars to go until my final reward. Which I'm pretty sure is going to be a weekend away alone – just me and my books. And a whole heap of chocolate.

JUNE

In June I had holidays. Well, half-holidays.

I was still supposed to work around two days a week but I had much more freedom with my time. I used that time to write and think a lot more.

I thought about what my skills and passions were. That reading and writing were things I really enjoyed and was good at and that not everyone felt the same way. I realised that I needed to value these things, not ignore them just because they were easy for me.

I thought about failure and success and was encouraged by a talk from Ken Costa,[20] where he stated that God would fulfil his objectives for actions we take in faith, even if it looks to us like we haven't been successful.

I was excited about the idea of starting each day feeling joyful about the day ahead. But I also couldn't really imagine it, couldn't imagine that there would be a job anywhere that was even slightly inside my comfort zone – a job that I wouldn't have to push myself to the limit to perform. And was it right to want to be inside the comfort zone all the time?

The thing I did the most in June was write. I finished the draft of my novel and sent it to my first readers for feedback. I wrote drafts of the blog posts I have put in this book. I even went to a writing craft seminar. And it was wonderful, refreshing, joyful. But was it going to work in the future? Was it what God wanted me to be doing? Or should I be pushing myself more?

CHAPTER EIGHT

Only do what you love?

I've talked a lot about saying *no*. But life is not all about saying *no*. Sometimes, we just need to say *yes*, and I'm going to share with you about something I said *yes* to. Something horribly hard.

Growing up, I was surrounded by family and friends. We often had people over for meals, or went to visit others. We always lived in a faith community – after a short period in a normal house on a normal street, my second home was a farm where drug addicts could come for rehabilitation; my next was a foster home for children; my next a missions community. We kids were taught, by the example of our parents, that relationships with other people were the most important thing in life.

There was one person that I always hated to visit.

Aunty Jill was not a relative, she was my mother's school friend. In those days we called all the adults Aunty and Uncle, regardless of whether they were related or not. There are some friends I still have now who have asked me could I please drop the honorific – it makes them feel old!

Jill is not one of those. She loved the title Aunty. She needed it.

Aunty Jill had a very hard upbringing. Her father was not around, and her mother was very ill for most of her childhood. Jill responded to this stress by becoming ill herself. I never remember her not being ill. Or needy. Or lonely.

When we would go to visit Jill would be lying in bed in her tiny unit.

She would pull me close to her scratchy chin and ample bosom and hug me for what seemed like forever. She would ask me questions about how I was, and whether I was happy, and she would make sure I gave the correct answer. She would give gifts – not gifts that suited us as such, but gifts she wanted to give. And then she would make sure we were properly grateful, that we said thank you, that we gave her a kiss and another interminably long hug.

She would take on the discipline of us children, making sure we behaved properly. If you said something she didn't agree with, she would try to make you back down and if you didn't, she would say, 'Fair enough.' A phrase I still rile at today.

But my mother was faithful in visiting her old friend, so we, as kids, were faithful too.

We moved away from Tasmania for a while, and with that, and the move back, and getting married and having children myself, I lost touch with Jill. I can't say I minded. I didn't even think about her.

Then one day, when I was taking my young son to the doctor, there was Jill in the waiting room. She was thrilled to see me. Thrilled to meet my kids. Gave us all long, scratchy hugs. Made sure that we would look her up – she had moved to a nursing home by this stage. Asked if I could help her with something.

I'm a sucker for being asked for help so I said *yes* and we reconnected.

Now I had to go and visit Jill myself, and she was thrilled that I did. Absolutely thrilled that I brought the kids with me. She would give us gifts again, hug us all again, manipulate us into staying longer than we ever planned to stay.

(I'd like to interrupt this story to state that I don't believe it's correct to make your children hug anyone they don't want to hug. I like the way that modern thinking stands on this issue. I wish I hadn't made my children hug Jill and I think I forced them less and less as time went on. A child's personal space is an important thing for them to protect.)

She would try to discipline my kids, to make them say what they didn't want to say, and that would make me angry. I was super angry that she was doing to my kids what she had done to me as a kid. I was super angry that I had to go and visit and that she wouldn't let me leave. I didn't want to be called her adopted niece or have the kids called her adopted great-niece and great-nephew.

But I would still go and visit.

Why? Because I believe that all human beings are valuable – not just the ones that are easy to love. I believe that God calls us to look after those who are in nursing homes, in prisons, in hospitals. Visiting Jill was horribly hard, but it fitted into my values, and I learned a lot from visiting her.

I learned about setting boundaries. I didn't force my kids to come with me and I would reward them after the visit if they did come. I let them see how angry I was and let them make their own decisions about what behaviour was appropriate and I think that helped them make their own decisions in similar situations.

I learned (from my daughter, Jess) how to say, 'I'm not comfortable with doing that Jill' when she would ask me to come and help her adjust her catheter or some such thing. I learned to say, and to help my children say what they really felt in answer to her questions, not the answer she wanted them to give.

I learned how to set a time limit for a visit, and how to leave when the time was up.

I learned how to decide how often to visit and stick to my decision no matter how much I was pressured to come more often.

I learned how to find out someone's love language (Jill's was gifts) and to speak it and to appreciate it being spoken even if it was not my own. (Mine is acts of service – a love language Jill simply couldn't speak.)

As my children grew up, they chose not to go and visit, and that was fine. And then, as they grew up a bit more, they chose to go and visit. And I was super proud of them for doing so.

Many self-help books and blogs encourage us to only do what we love. They would say that my visit to Jill was a waste of time and emotional energy. That I should have crossed her off my list of activities to do and should have found instead something that built me up, that encouraged me, that energised me. But as hard as my visits to Jill were, I was strengthened by the experience.

When we look for a way to simplify our lives, the agenda for what goes on our list of things to do (and what gets crossed off) needs to be a greater one than 'do I enjoy this activity?'. Many things are worth doing, even when they are not enjoyable.

Instead of asking if something is enjoyable, I think we need to ask whether it sits in our values. Whether it is our responsibility. Jill was, partly, my responsibility. I needed to step up to the plate.

I don't have a ministry to people in nursing homes. I am not one of those amazing angels of people who adopt the lost and lonely, the poorest in our community, and reach out to them. Meeting those people at Jill's birthday parties over the years was one of the rewards of reaching out to Jill.

But Jill fell in my purview. She had very few friends, a very boring life, and she needed the connection to our family. I needed to put aside my selfishness for half an hour twice a year to reach out to her. Even though it was exhausting. And yes, I whinged about her a fair bit. Like I said, I'm no angel.

When looking at what to cut out of your life, what to say *no* to, you may have a situation like I had with Jill. Something that is not fun, not rewarding, and does not help you invest in your ultimate dream. Most of the time we say *no* to these things, but be careful that you are not missing the chance to sacrifice your life, to take up your cross, to build the kingdom of God.

Sometimes it is better to do the things we don't love. Sometimes it's right.

CHAPTER NINE

Do you really enjoy this?

Here's the flip side to the last chapter: Just because something is hard for you, doesn't mean it's automatically the right thing to do.

This may not be news to you, but I tell you, it has been big news for me.

I went to my cousin's thirtieth birthday party last year. He had invited all of his church friends, and all of his family. He had invited everyone. He goes to a different church to me and I knew many people there on a Facebook-friend basis, but there were not a lot of my close friends going.

The party was held in a brewery, a big barn of a place. It was meant to run all afternoon. There was an open fire, nibbles to eat, drinks you could buy. He didn't plan many activities – just the cutting of the cake and a few speeches. The rest of the time was to be spent milling around and chatting.

Now, as an introvert, that kind of afternoon is … difficult. An afternoon of unplanned small talk with people I didn't know well. I didn't want to go. But this was my cousin, and it was his thirtieth, and I love him and his family. So I made plans to turn up late, and to leave early. And to try my best while I was there.

This is the thing that shocked me: When my cousin got up to make his speech he said that he had planned the afternoon to be what it was because it contained all of the things that he loved.

Can you hear me? He planned an afternoon of pain and suffering because this is what he loved.

For him, the party was pure joy from start to finish.

For me, not so much. Although, I am exaggerating about the pain and suffering.

Still, that was a bit of a breakthrough moment for me.

Somewhere down in the depths of my being I believed that there were types of events that no-one loved. That everyone went to these events because they loved the person for whom the event was held and they wanted to show their affection to that person.

Some parties I really enjoy, and some not so much. I think it's something to do with the ratio of people I know well to people I don't, or the amount of small talk required, or maybe even the activities we're doing.

In the past, there were parties that I only attended out of a sense of love and duty. They were a socially acceptable method of showing my affection and regard to a special person. They were not events to be enjoyed.

Once I realised that people actually go to these events because they enjoy them, I felt released to not attend them if I didn't want to. Or at least to only turn up for a short time.

I understand this is an introvert issue, but I have put myself through discomfort and exhaustion time after time out of a misplaced sense of duty. There have been many parties and occasions that I just should have missed. Though I really love to be invited.

Now, if I feel like I need to show my appreciation for someone, I might find a different way of doing it. I might send a card or a present. I might invite them for one-on-one coffee at another time.

I am learning to take a different stance.

I am learning to think about whether I would enjoy an outing. If yes, then I go. If no, then I need to think about it a bit more. There may be other reasons that I would benefit from attending, or that I would benefit others by attending. But sometimes I feel free to leave it to the people who would enjoy going. The people who actively look for these opportunities.

Learning that other people actually like parties helped me to understand that I didn't have to like parties. It helped me to learn to say *no* when I am invited to a party that I don't want to go to. Other people will be there and will enjoy it. The same with big church activities (see the previous story about the high tea for Mother's Day), or school fairs, or party plan parties, or big science festivals, or the morning tea roster. There are some things I am not going to force myself to attend anymore. And I'm not going to feel guilty about it.

There are things that suit me to do, that don't suit others and vice versa.

An example is the way that I volunteer at church.

The other day I was having a coffee with my friend Dess and I mentioned how I had been asked to provide dessert for a particular course our church is running.

She looked at me and said, 'Food isn't really your thing though, is it?'

'No,' I said, 'but anyone can help with the serving and clearing up.'

She just shook her head at me.

We chatted a bit more, and later at home I found my invitation email and replied to say that no, I wouldn't be helping out with this particular task, and suggested someone else to ask, who might enjoy it.

I have volunteered in a few different capacities. I have cleaned the toilets. I have worked the computer to put the words on the screen. I have handed out news sheets and taken up offerings. I understand that serving takes many forms and that being part of an organisation like a church involves serving the organisation.

I know that we should be willing to serve the Lord in whatever capacity he calls us to. That cleaning the toilets is no less of a service than leading the services.

For a while I thought that meant that I should clean toilets, or serve morning tea. Not only that I should be willing to take the most uncomfortable job, but that I should actively seek out the most uncomfortable job.

But now I think differently.

The way I volunteer at the moment is by leading services. Around once a month I stand in front of about 300 people and MC the morning worship. I give the notices, announce the kids' spot, pray, generally link the whole thing together.

I enjoy it. It's tiring, but it's worthwhile, satisfying, joyful. And it's something I find I can do. Well, I think I can. I made the same comment to someone over coffee after a service once and she said, 'Who told you that?' Anyway, I find that leading the service is something I am well suited to. It is more within my abilities to lead once a month than to serve tea and coffee afterwards.

There is nothing inherently holy or worthy or wonderful about forcing yourself to perform activities that you don't enjoy. I don't believe that we are meant to be miserable and exhausted all the time. If you are not enjoying an activity, it may be a sign that you should stop doing it. Let someone else take the reins – it might be just what they are looking for. Some people absolutely love being on the cleaning roster – it fills a part of their love for order and cleanliness and gives them joy. Others love serving morning tea, saying good morning to every single person who attended church that day. Still others get a kick out of running the technology for the service.

It is good to be willing to serve in any capacity but it is surely better to serve in a way that suits your personality and talents. To take that load that others don't want and to give them the chance to do something that they would like to do. I am not saying that you should put off serving until you get the chance to do the one thing that you would be perfectly suited to. But I am saying that if we all work at the things we love, there's a good chance that all the jobs would be taken care of and we would all be happier and healthier people.

JULY

In July I thought about the time and effort I was investing in my writing. I wondered whether it would all be worth it. In God's economy things are a bit different and I wondered if the point was that my failures and pathetic writings would be valuable just as an encouragement to someone else to start walking in faith. Would the point of the exercise just be that I learn how to fail?

Finishing holidays and returning to work was difficult. It took one day to feel completely exhausted again. To feel like I was losing my mind. I wondered how I had allowed myself to be so overextended, so overloaded.

At the same time I was scared to leave the job. Every time I told someone I was leaving I felt more crazy for doing it. Who was I to think that I could make a living from my writing? Who was I to think that other people would want to read what I write?

I wanted a concrete sign from God that this was what He wanted me to do, but at the same time I felt that God was wanting me to walk in faith. And I had the peace between Moz and myself – that would have to do.

Walking in faith is not easy. Everyone's stories are told at the end, when you see it all coming together and you understand how necessary the struggles are on the way through. But when you're in the middle, jumping out of the boat, the journey is not that easy.

CHAPTER TEN

Appointments and margin

Imagine this: You are at a meeting with your supervisor and your student. The meeting is to look at the student's past year of work and make a plan for the next few months. You are the person who is responsible for guiding the student through the next section of their work. You need to be totally present, thinking of all the options and issues that may appear in the future.

The meeting starts at 10.30 and you have scheduled a coffee with a friend at 11.30. The meeting should have only taken half an hour but things are difficult to understand and nut out, conversations go around in circles, and any time you try to clarify, another option or issue rears its ugly head. As the clock ticks on, you become more and more distracted, wondering if there is a way to get a message to your friend without looking bad. You cease to concentrate on the job in hand, you are now doing bad work as well as feeling stressed.

Or here's another example. You pick up your mother each Friday morning at 9 am, have a coffee with her and drop her off at her church for her prayer meeting at 10.15. That works well most weeks, but this week you have a doctor's appointment in town at 10.30. Once again, sitting in the café with your mother you are constantly checking your watch, the problem is not getting from the church to town, the problem is parking. If it all goes smoothly you'll be fine, but if there's a lot of people in the multi-storey car-park you'll be ten minutes late for the appointment and who knows? They may just cancel, assuming you're not coming. You don't hear a word your mother says as your brain visualises the car park, the parking meters near the surgery, the road on the way there. You hustle your mother out of the car at the prayer meeting, your stress levels are through the roof.

These two situations are situations I have narrowly avoided.

Marcia Ramsland,[25] a professional organiser, suggests strongly that we put space around our appointments. And I agree with her.

Here's how I solved my problems:

When I found that I had a 10.30 meeting before the regular coffee date with my friend Naomi I sent her a text message. I told her that I would be in a meeting and I had no idea how long it would take. I asked if we could have a bit of flexibility as to when we met for coffee – if I could send her another message when the meeting finished so we could meet up after that. She was totally accommodating. Now I could concentrate when I needed to and I could still meet my friend. The first meeting went for an hour and a half so I was very glad I had acted.

My mother came up with the answer to my second situation. I told her about the doctor's appointment and she suggested that we go into town and have coffee near the surgery. Then she took a taxi to her prayer meeting – easily done as the taxi stand was near the café in town and the taxi didn't have to find parking.

In general, I try to give my self at least ten minutes between appointments. Half an hour if possible. As much wriggle room as I can. Travel takes time, meetings go overtime, parking isn't always available close to the place that you need to be.

There are always little jobs that you can squeeze into the half hour between appointments. I take my journal with me everywhere so I can write in it. I also tend to take my kindle so I can read if I have time. Or I'll take a research article that I need to work my way through. (I have a large handbag – can you tell?) That half-hour can be used to give you time to think about life for a bit, time to ponder and dream.

On the other hand, overlapping appointments are going to cause you stress as well as annoying the person you are late for. It's not worth it.

What does this have to do with saying no?

Again, it's having those rules in place for yourself. If someone asks you to attend a meeting, come for coffee, or do a task that will overlap with another meeting or appointment scheduled on your calendar then the answer just has to be *no* – or at least not today. Don't try to squeeze the most possible into your day. Give yourself breathing space. It will make your life better.

Part of the problem is that we get a kick out of being busy. We feel important when we are busy.

When someone asks how we are, we sigh and say, 'I'm so busy.'

We race from activity to activity, we have no time to cook, no time to read, no time to stop and ponder the imponderables of life. It's not good, we know it, but we find it difficult to change.

The book I've found most helpful when thinking about my busy life is *Margin: Restoring Emotional, Physical, Financial, and Time Reserves to Overloaded Lives* by Richard Swenson.[23]

Swenson is convinced that many illnesses of our age are caused by our rushing, overloaded, frantic, busy lives. I can well believe him.

He has come up with the idea of allowing margin in our lives so that we can have space to spill over when we need to. Just as good money management means living within your means, making sure you have enough money to cover your expenses and a little left over for when things don't go according to plan, Swenson suggests we budget our time with margin built in – time to do what we need to do, and some time left over. Then the margin in our time can be used to reach out to others, to connect with our families, to give us space to be able to give of ourselves.

Now I must be a bit daft, but when I first read that I thought that it meant that I needed to squeeze yet more into my day. That I would have to give time to family and friends, have more people over for dinner, and so on, as well as all that I was already doing. It made me panic a bit – if there's one thing I can't do, it's squeeze more into my day.

But no, he's suggesting that we take activities out of our days and as a regular thing we have space that is not allocated. This space would usually be used for regeneration, for relaxation and rest, but if an emergency comes up we would use that space to adjust for the emergency. We could drop everything to help someone out because the only thing we would be dropping is our regular evening in front of the fire reading a book.

Ramsland is also worried about how much we are trying to fit into each week. Her advice is not to go out any more than four evenings a week. I find that is excellent advice to follow. In fact, I don't do evenings very well, so even four evenings a week is beyond me.

I've found that I needed to work out how much margin I needed each week and book that in without feeling guilty about it. I needed to decide that time for me to rest and rejuvenate, to walk and read, to look after myself and my family, that time is just as important as meeting with, looking after, and taking care of other people and other people's priorities.

But I needed to book it in to my calendar.

Once it is booked in, I can say *no* easily to many things because I have made the decision already. In the past. Not in the present when I am feeling under pressure from the person asking me.

So I can just look at my calendar and say, 'I'm all booked, sorry, can we do Wednesday week instead?'

It's a much better way to go than overloading yourself, stressing about it, and resenting the person for needing the time that you just don't have to give.

And also, if there is a genuine crisis, you have time to be there.

One of my blog readers, when reading about budgeting our time, commented, 'Bills just keep coming.' And I can see what he's saying. We can go through times of crisis where money is tight, bills keep coming, and we have no way to get through without going into debt or something – something we would prefer to avoid. We can go through the same thing with time.

There are times when the appointments come thick and fast. We are wrapping up a special project at work, or renovating the house before Christmas. I remember feeling this way at the end of my honours year. There is a deadline and we need to push to get there. We fill up every spare corner of our calendar. We are stretched and we have to keep going, overwhelmed, but we just must keep going.

You know, this is fine for a short period, but if your life feels like this every single week then I suggest that you might need to make some hard decisions and remove some of the tasks you have given yourself. You are not meant to keep going at breakneck speed forever. We need rest. It will be worth the time spent to look at your time budget and get it under control. I promise.

AUGUST

In August I felt frazzled, overwhelmed, exhausted, and busy, powerful, important; and at times rested, bored, grateful, happy, and then tired, trapped, and angry. I had days at work where it was not humanly possible to fit in everything that needed to be done, but I felt useful and needed. I had appointments and meetings outside of work and tried to keep working on my writing. I had evenings at home spent in front of the fire, reading, chatting to Moz, playing crib, even singing along with him to his piano playing.

There was no balance. Work was crazy, and harder to do because I'd made the decision to leave. But interspersed in the work days were islands of rest. Sometimes enforced rest because of the flu, sometimes just conscious rest.

I was scared that looking forward to the future was just being naïve and closing my eyes to reality, and that things would never be better than they already were. I practised living 'in the moment' and I was blessed by conversations with friends who helped me bear my burdens.

I made it through the month, gasping for air, and determined that next winter I would do better. I was very happy to leave the winter behind.

CHAPTER ELEVEN

Seasons

As I said in chapter five, one of the things I did when I was trying to figure out what to say *no* to was to make a mind-map of my life. I divided it up into sections: family, church, work, writing, and health. In each section I put the activities that I wanted to include and make time for and I used that map as a method of saying *no* to those things that didn't fit in the segments.

It was a good way of seeing clearly what the priorities were in my life, and of figuring out what things just didn't fit into my priorities. A way of looking at what I valued, and a way of testing each opportunity as it came.

Just a few months after I filled in this mind-map I could already see things that no longer fitted my life. For example, one of the planned tasks under 'work' was to apply for a new position that I knew would be advertised at my workplace. This position was an opportunity I had been waiting for for years. I thought it would fulfil my desire for permanency and security and when I drew up the mind-map I was ready to go for it.

In the, I don't know, three or four months after I completed the mind-map, my ideas completely changed. I no longer wanted to apply for the job. I wouldn't have accepted it if it were handed to me on a silver platter. I was ready to change direction and so grateful that I wasn't locked into a long-term position.

I often get sucked into what I call 'The Enid Blyton Mindset'. The idea that if you get everything under control, get into the right school, job, or relationship, or have a certain amount of money saved, or figure out the right exercise routine, or somehow just get every area of your life just right, then you'll live 'Happily Ever After'.

Of course, it doesn't work like that. Things are constantly changing. Your exercise routine might work really well until you get sick, or the amount of money you have for a buffer might be exactly right until your car breaks down and it all gets used up. Life is particularly skilled at throwing spanners in the works. We need to be flexible, constantly changing, constantly growing.

Some seasons of life are particularly hard. One of the seasons of life that I found especially draining was when my children were small. As much as I loved my children (and still do), it was all I could do just to get through each day. I lived in a constant state of exhausted fog. I don't think that I could have done any writing when the kids were small, even though it is the thing that gives me life and joy now. It just would not have fitted into that season of my life.

The thing I'm trying to say is that our needs and wants change over time. It's not that we have one perfect life set-up that we are struggling towards and when we get there it will be bliss. No, I think we need to be flexible with ourselves and take the time to have a good hard look at where we are every so often so that we can adjust our list of priorities. What was once so very important may now be dropped off the list. If a new priority (maybe taking care of ageing parents) comes on to the list, other priorities (the morning tea roster at church) might have to be knocked off. Or it might just be time, like it is now for me, to deliberately change your life so that a new major priority can get major chunks of time.

What do you think of the idea of seasons? Is it time for a change in your life? Or are you just hanging on to see a certain season through and wondering if things will ever change?

You might be saying, 'OK Ruth, that's all well and good, but I had plans, good plans, and I've put aside time to follow them, and I was going fine down the road and I've suddenly hit a massive road block. What now?'

What happens when life says *no* to you? When you've done all the right things, followed all the steps for success, held on until the season seemed right, gone for it, and then… BAM. When the amount of flexibility you need to deal with what life throws at you is about the same as a roller-skater going under the limbo pole that's 10 cm off the ground?

I haven't really gone through this myself, but you might be able to take some tips from what my mother has gone through.

My mother is a concert pianist. As kids, we took it for granted. Didn't everyone go and watch their mother perform? Hadn't everyone's mother been recorded and played on ABC radio? No, of course not, we knew that, but it takes a while for kids to appreciate how special their own mother's talent is, I think. I found out recently that at 15 years of age my mum won a concerto contest and played a movement of Beethoven's First Piano Concerto with the Tasmanian Symphony Orchestra. That's pretty impressive if you ask me, and there were many more triumphs to follow.

Mum's playing sometimes took a front seat, like when she and Dad moved to the USA for ten years to work with the Christian Performing Arts Fellowship,[26] and sometimes it took more of a back seat, like when she was raising us kids. It was always a joint decision between Mum and Dad as to which direction they took their lives.

But some years ago now, when Mum and Dad were in the USA, they noticed an increased stiffness and weakness in Mum's right arm and hand. It didn't go away so they came back to Australia to start looking into medical options. Mum was diagnosed with Parkinson's Disease.

It was really frustrating for her. She could still play beautifully and better than most people, but she couldn't play to the standard that she wanted to. The concerts and recordings were taken away from her and it definitely wasn't her choice.

Sometimes seasons change for us and we don't want them to at all. But we still have a choice as to how we deal with that situation.

Don't get me wrong. You need to grieve when you have something like that ripped away from you. It's not fair, and it's definitely not fun. But, there is something you can do. I'll show you what Mum did.

She changed her focus. She still played piano, but she chose to use this moment to focus on another part of music that was very close to her heart – choral work.

At the moment Mum leads two choral groups and is part of a third. One choir leads the singing at the church where she is music minister, one choir performs in old people's homes and regional festivals and all sorts of places, one choir does more semi-professional oratorio works. Mum is still surrounded by music and still giving so much to the people around her.

I have another beautiful friend Mandy who has been crippled with chronic fatigue. She is unable to work, unable to do anything most days but sit in the garden and occasionally walk to the end of her driveway. But somehow she still manages to post little tidbits and photos on Facebook that enrich the lives of those of us who read them.

Sometimes life says *no* to you. The trick seems to be finding the new thing in the new season that can give you life and fulfilment. Being grateful for what you still have (no matter how small) and being able to reach out to others through that.

Nobody wants these seasons. They are no fun. They are not what we planned and not what we'd do if we were in charge. If you are going through something like this I am so sorry.

I hope that you can find a spark to help you through it, maybe a change of plan, maybe a little joy that you can give to others, or maybe there's another way of coping that I don't know about – I'd love to hear from you about it. I hope that I can remember some of this (or that someone will gently remind me) if I become the one stuck in the roadblock.

SEPTEMBER

In September I worked harder than I ever have in my life. Many things coincided: the organisation and hosting of a visiting lecturer at the university, a lab day for my chemistry class, leading the church service one Sunday, the school fair, my supervisor leaving on holiday and putting me in charge of the well-being of three PhD students. I felt overwhelmed and unwell for most of the month.

My body stopped relaxing. I had wakeful nights. My brain wouldn't stop thinking. I was always in a state of preparedness for the next big thing.

But I got through. And as we reached the end of the month and school holidays came in sight, I breathed a sigh of relief and looked back at the achievements of the month with satisfaction.

I realised that when I decided to leave the university, I started to relax more about the work there. To stress less about getting ahead in my career. That relaxation helped me to look at the workplace more dispassionately and to understand how the system worked and what needed to be done to get ahead in that workplace. Temptation came my way in the form of some professors encouraging me to fill out a fellowship application. They were sure I could get funding and that I could stay. But I had decided to leave.

I spent a lot of the month wondering how the new thing was going to work and whether I was just kidding myself – living in a fairytale. Then one day I woke up believing that I could do it. That I could be a Christian author of non-fiction books on things like time management, and fiction books like murder mysteries. I believed it.

PERSONAL CHALLENGES

ROAD MARATHON vs. NETFLIX MARATHON

CHAPTER TWELVE

When to push yourself

Earlier this year I was privileged to host a visiting lecturer to our institution. I have been trying for some time to be an advocate for gender equity in our workplace and the idea of a Women's Lectureship was suggested to me – bringing a role model down to Tasmania to encourage our female PhD students. I won't go into all the reasons here, but I jumped at the chance to organise this visit.

Professor Michelle Coote[27] agreed to visit with us for a week and I dived into the organisation. I had no idea just what was required for the hosting of a visiting lecturer. There were the flights and accommodation of course; I didn't book those but I did liaise with our office staff to make sure we got it right. Then I had to decide on when to hold the public lecture, when to hold the seminar, when to hold the gender equity forum. And where.

And then things got a little more complicated. After choosing a time for the public lecture, booking the lecture room (and making sure that we'd booked it with a little leeway so that we could easily get set up), and advertising on all the university websites and Facebook and, well, everywhere that I could think of, we found out that we had cleverly booked the lecture room for 7am rather than 7pm. And that the lecture room was already booked for another group at 7pm. And that the other booking couldn't be changed.

PANIC!

Then try not to let the panic show, and try to calm every-one down, and don't let Michelle know that anything had gone wrong with the plan, and head for plan B.

We had a couple of options for plan B and we went with the lecture room that was available and closest to the original room. The only problems being that 1) it was a much larger room than we really wanted so our crowd would look tiny, and 2) it was booked right up until our opening time and the group before us would be having wine and cheese in the foyer as our attendees were coming in to our (wine and cheese-less) lecture. But it was the best available option so we went with it.

The night arrived. However, the pizza that we had ordered to eat for tea in-between work and the lecture did not arrive, so I was fairly hungry. What did arrive was the rain and the bitter cold. Which made me wonder if any audience members would decide to arrive. But we battled on.

The lecture happened and it went well. Of course. Michelle is a professional and her research is fascinating. We had a reasonable audience (more than five anyway). We even managed to pick up a couple of attendees from the wine and cheese event. They came and sat in our lecture with their glasses of wine and hopefully learned something about self-healing polymers and solar cells.

The next day was the gender equity forum and I was busy buying cakes and snacks to encourage people to come and trying to fit that in around my regular work. And the day after that was the seminar that I was also chairing, and the lunch afterwards.

It was a busy week. I didn't have time to breathe. There was definitely no work-life balance that week. No gaps between appointments. No time to evaluate whether or not this or that was what I wanted to do.

But I am very glad I took on the challenge. Really grateful for the opportunity and the lessons learned.

The term 'work-life balance' can sound static. Like it's a set point that we're trying to find that we can set our thermostat to and have the same balance all the time. But life isn't static. Even when our days are good, life has its ups and downs. Maybe it's better to try to find a work-life rhythm than a work-life balance. (No, that idea isn't my own, but I can't remember where I heard it first.)

As a normal way of being, I think it is right to build margin into our days, to set aside time to follow our goals, to build in some down-time, to make sure we have some peace.

But sometimes it is right to push ourselves – to squeeze more into our days, to stretch a little outside our comfort zones, to try to reach a little bit further. Some days bring us an opportunity to work hard and be busy and go for it a bit. And the margin and the self-care built into the regular times will give you the energy to push yourself when it is necessary.

I guess the question is, how do you tell which are the good moments to push yourself, and which are extras where we should say *no*?

I don't know the total answer to this, of course, you are you and I am me and what we need to decide are two different things, but there's a few things we can think through when making this kind of decision.

One is to get a reasonable estimate of the amount of time we have to give to the project. This takes practice of course. I had no idea how much time would be swallowed by Michelle's visit, but I know now. I was very grateful that my other projects could be shunted to the side somewhat when Michelle was down so that I could give the lectureship the time it required without totally burning out. I think I could have helped myself with the time management by finding someone else who had done something similar and asking them for an estimate.

Another question to ask is whether this event will bring you closer to your life goals or whether it's just busy-work. If you find your day is regularly getting built in by endless tasks that don't seem to get you anywhere that you want to go, then maybe it's best to start delegating or organising or somehow getting that busy-work off your plate. Easier said than done, I know, but if you don't even recognise the problem then you're unlikely to find any answers.

And finally, are you doing this out of selfish ambition? Is the only reason you're taking on this event or project that the outcome will make you look good? I know that some of my readers might not like the fact that I'm making a distinction here, but I'm all about going for it to reach your goals (ambition) but really not into doing it to make you look good to others (selfish ambition). Working yourself to death because it makes you look good to others is a really bad idea in my book.

Anyway, to summarise, yes, I think there are good reasons to push yourself sometimes. But I also think that these should be short-term sprints and not a way of life. And I would hope that they are in service of others.

OCTOBER

The clouds started to clear. The semester finished with only exam marking to go. The countdown on my calendar was over.

Then the grief hit. Halfway home after giving my last lesson I started to cry and the tears just didn't stop. University life was my big dream and desire for a long time and I needed to say a proper goodbye to that dream before picking up the next one. My cousin helped me by saying, 'Remember that choosing not to pursue this path anymore does not invalidate what it gave you.' Solid advice.

But at the same time as I was filled with grief, I felt like I was entering the promised land. All those scriptures really rang true. 'As you enter the land ... be careful that you do not forget the Lord.'[28] My brain started to fill with the things I could do in my new lifestyle: writing, an editing business, time with family and friends, working around the house, exercise. Would there be enough time in the day to do all that? Would I now have the energy?

I was ready to go. Let's get started on the new thing. Surely now I can start. But no, not yet. There were still work hours that needed to be completed. Still jobs to do.

And lastly, in this very emotional month, I was scared. Begging God, 'Please let this work. Please. Please.' And talking myself back from the edge of terror by telling myself that I hadn't started yet, that I knew what to do, that I was very productive in my half-holidays. I wasn't sure whether to be stressed or relaxed, happy or sad. The only thing I was sure about was that I was still tired.

CHAPTER THIRTEEN

Am I just lazy?

I've talked a lot about saying *no* to things. About having days alone where my introvert self can recharge; about saying *no* to some requests and not even feeling guilty; about leaving some church or work activities to others; about rewarding myself for telling people *no*; about making sure that I'm not too busy and that I have time to do the things that really matter to me. And all of this is good, at least I think it's good and that's why I'm sharing it with you.

But there's often a bit of a nagging worry in the back of my mind. I ask myself, 'Am I just lazy?'

I mean, if I compare myself to my friend Naomi who runs her own tutoring business then I definitely look lazy – she works from 8am to 7pm tutoring school children and then spends her evenings writing reports and such. She's amazing! Or how about my friend Megan, who gets up at dark-o-clock to go jogging before getting her kids off to school and then going to work herself. She also looks after her elderly mother and helps out at church things.

But I'm sure I could compare myself to others who have different priorities or different health levels to me and think that I'm doing pretty well.

Comparisonitis, Joanna Penn calls it. It's a deadly disease, sure to stop any endeavour. It's a seriously bad idea to compare your life to another's. The very best it can do is puff you up with pride, and that's not a good thing.

It is more likely to destroy you as you try to meet some unattainable ideal.

So, how then do you figure out if you are making the best use of the time and energy levels that you have been given in your day?

I found some very good advice in Kristine Rusch's book *Goals and Dreams*.[29] She says to set a daily goal and try to achieve it for a week:

> If you never reach the goal, figure out if the problem is that you weren't putting in enough time, that you didn't have enough time to give ... or if the goal is just too hard to achieve in a single day for you. Then, set a new goal and try that for a week. Work until you find one you have to stretch just a little to achieve, but make sure it is one you can achieve.

I think this is fantastic advice. It requires being honest with yourself but that's a good thing too.

I am really blessed in that I have a husband who will be honest with me. He sees what I do and what I don't, and he can give me feedback to let me know whether I'm being lazy, or whether I'm taking a well-deserved break from some hard work. Sometimes it's just so helpful to have someone else say, 'No, rest, you deserve it'. But even in my incredibly blessed situation I can feel like he's not seeing the full picture and that I'm just being lazy. So I also need to self-assess, to set goals I can reach in a day, in a week. And to constantly reassess.

I love how Rusch says that goals can be reassessed on a constant basis. What works one week or month may not work the next. If you are reaching goals too easily then you may need to set the bar higher. If you are never achieving your goals and just getting frustrated then you may need to lower your expectations of yourself for this season, and this energy level. Just because you set a goal for yourself doesn't mean it's set in stone. Just like pilots are constantly correcting their course when flying a plane or piloting a ship, we also need to constantly correct our life course and make sure we're on track. Reassess, realign, set another goal and try to reach it.

It can be good to have someone to be accountable to. Someone to whom you have stated your goal and will report back to. That may help you keep honest so that you're not kidding yourself about your energy levels or time commitments. You need someone who can hold up a mirror to you that is not too distorted, and can help you to see the truth about yourself.

So are you just lazy? Am I? I think the answer is so much more complex than that.

I love productivity books. Like, I really love them. I think I read them more than I read novels. Maybe. I love any book with a journal, pen, and cup of coffee on the cover. It's an addiction, really.

I'm not sure that it's healthy.

What if I'm reading these productivity books just because by reading them I can feel like I'm being productive without actually doing anything?

The interesting thing is that when I started writing the series of blogs that eventually became this book, I realised that I didn't need to set aside time to do a whole lot of research – I had already done the research as I read all the productivity books. I could now just put it all together, put my take on it, and make a series of my own.

I think it's easy to feel lazy when you're spending time doing things you love doing. I love to read. If I spend the day reading a book I feel very lazy and unproductive indeed, but for others the exact same day would have been a day of hard work.

I can write a thousand words and again feel like I've done nothing. I love to write. But as I do that day after day, I can put together a book and others will feel like I've been very productive.

Doing what you love is not necessarily laziness.

Doing something 'just for fun' is not necessarily a waste of time.

Laziness is such a subjective thing.

Recovery is another thing that masquerades as laziness – but isn't.

As I write this I am sitting on my couch recovering after attending the Oliebollen Festival.[30] The Oliebollen Festival (for those of you who don't live in Kingston, Tasmania) is our school fair. It's quite a big one, as school fairs go. I once read a tourist book that mentioned two things about my town of Kingston – the Australian Antarctic Division, and the Oliebollen Festival. There is a display of vintage cars on the oval, there are side-show rides, the Navy Band often comes and plays for us, there is the book stall, the white elephant, the auction, the plants, the baby animals, and of course the food. Oliebollen are Dutch donuts – deep fried dough with fruit dotted through and sprinkled with icing sugar – very much an annual treat for me.

So I went to the festival but I knew that after a couple of hours or so at the fair I would need to spend quite some hours chilling out. The festival is fun, it's loud, there are heaps of people to say hello to, and afterwards I need to stop and sit in a quiet place. I've come back home and sat on the couch. I might stay here for a while.

It's not just festivals that make me feel tired like this. I am like this after church, I am like this after judging a poster session at the graduate research conference, I am like this after University Open Day, I am like this after every large event. I even feel tired after giving a lecture, and that has been part of my job at least two days a week for 26 weeks of the year.

I have seen a meme that says 'Adult life is just telling each other how tired we are until one of us dies.' So I know that I'm not the only one who feels tired most of the time.

Some of my issue is health-related and I have spent a fair bit of time looking into that. And some of it is introversion – time with people is tiring and I need time alone to recharge.

The thing is, the recharge time is necessary for me. It's not me being lazy or not coping. It's the fact that if I don't take the time to recharge, then I will end up not coping at all.

As part of my time budget I need to book in recharge time after an event. And when I look at what I am saying *yes* to and what I am saying *no* to, I need to take into account the number of people at the event and how exhausted I am likely to be afterwards. It's not slackness, it's just the way it is.

One of the comments on my blog reminded me that we learn that the busier we are the 'better' we are as people, and suggested that we could look at the example of the counter cultural life of Winnie the Pooh. I totally agree, though I'm not talking the Disney version. The original A A Milne books poke gentle fun at our self-importance and busy-ness. Rabbit holds a mirror to our lives and asks, 'is it really that important?' and Winnie the Pooh and Piglet show us that friendship and a 'little smackerel of something' might be the most important thing of all.[31]

NOVEMBER

I find myself alone in a park overlooking the river. The water is completely calm and the slight breeze is fluttering a flag flying above a boat repair place in front of me. I can hear birds singing and gulls crying to each other. I slow down enough to watch birds sipping nectar from flowers, and then slow down more to notice the insect life crawling around me. Then I think of the insects crawling on me and the moment gets significantly less restful. I write for a bit, then go to meet a friend for coffee.

November is all about slowing down. I feel so much relief as the teaching completely stops. I also feel a little lost. Time feels loose and difficult to pin down. My self-confidence lowers as I'm no longer busy and important, but just me. I need a new routine but I realise that this won't be possible until after the Christmas madness passes.

I have more brain space. I am exercising more, eating better, getting little tasks done that have been weighing on my mind for (literally) years. I swing back and forth between hope that my new life will be wonderful, and fear that it will end up being just the same as my old life and that I'll never cope with anything.

I need to take the time to adjust, and move forward, one foot in front of the other.

MUCH BETTER...

CHAPTER FOURTEEN

Rest

OK, let's get serious now. We all know that we only have 24 hours in a day, 168 hours in a week, and that how you live your moments is how you live your days. And therefore, everything we do needs to be full of meaning, pushing our lives (however incrementally) in the right direction, and mindful. Right?

Well…

Depending on your understanding of what I've just written, there could be something missing from the picture. What about play? You know, the act of doing something fun, alone or with friends or family, that doesn't go anywhere, that isn't part of any great plan. What about board games, or throwing a frisbee on the beach, or building things from Lego?

My grandmother lived to the ripe old age of ninety-nine and eleven twelfths. She just missed her hundredth birthday by about five weeks. In her later years she took up painting. She had a little table set up with her watercolours and brushes and she painted all the time. Mostly English or Australian countrysides, pictures that she liked from magazines or photographs. But the paintings were not great masterpieces. And they were never going to be great masterpieces. No matter how much she painted, it was not going anywhere. None of them would be money makers. It didn't matter. That's not why she painted.

In this era of entrepreneurship, we are often encouraged to monetise our hobbies and passions and I can understand that, I'm trying to do that right now with writing. But I think we can go too far and start to stress that all our activities must be worthwhile in some sense. That if we're reading, the books must be great literature that will expand our brain. If we're on the computer we must be working or reading the news. That our outside play must be exercise. That our baking must be time spent investing in our children.

I think it's important to put time aside just for play.

I'm not good at this, mind you. I've tried various hobbies in my life and dropped most of them because I couldn't bear spending money on something that didn't lead anywhere. I write lists of jobs for my weekend and feel righteous if I've accomplished them all. And I'm not good with spontaneous happenings. I don't spontaneously go and watch a movie, or invite friends for a night of board games.

So I've come up with a compromise. On the weekends I set aside part of Saturday as time for planned spontaneity. Moz and I may take that time and go for a drive somewhere and visit touristy shops or have lunch in a café or find a beach to take a walk along. We enjoy these mini-adventures. But we also might not go. Depending.

I'm also reading more – novels, memoir, whatever takes my fancy. Not research for my writing, but just anything I like. And I watch a little TV and I surf a little Facebook.

I know that, like anything, this can get out of balance. We've been told for years that we're all watching too much TV. And social media can be a huge time-suck as well. Boundaries need to be put in place and some of our play needs to not involve screens at all. Non-screen play tends to be more refreshing, I think. And most of what we do should move us in the right direction.

But I think it's a good idea when you're setting up your time budget, to allocate a little time to play. It's a necessary part of life.

"I'LL MAKE MYSELF INDISPENSABLE"

When I started working at the university on short-term contracts, I had a plan. I would say *yes* to as many things as possible, and make myself indispensable, and then they would have to keep renewing my contracts and I would be as good as permanent.

I didn't say it was a good plan.

You see the problem with thinking like that is that when the time came this year when I really needed to take a break, I didn't feel like I could because I had made myself indispensable. I felt like things would fall over if I took so much as a week off. And so I came close to exhaustion.

I think it must be a personality-type thing for me, or something. I like being friends with people, but what I really like is being needed. I love being the one people turn to in a crisis. I love it so much, until I don't. I love it until I am tired and I really need a break, but there's no one else who can take the load.

It's pride, people. Plain and simple.

None of us can carry that burden.

I'm not meant to be the one solving everyone's problems. I am not meant to be the sole provider of friendship to people, or the sole dispenser of wisdom. It works much better if everyone does their little bit than if I feel (even mistakenly) that it all depends on me.

One of the things that can help stop me from continually falling into this trap is the practice of regularly taking one day off a week. It's a discipline that helps put everything back into order. That gives a regular reset of the brain.

When I was working full-time, a Sabbath for me meant a day when I didn't do any paid work. I would make sure I didn't do any work at all as a statement of faith that God would either make it OK that the work didn't get done, or make me cope with the fact that disaster happened.

It was amazing how little disaster did happen. In fact, I can't think of one time when taking a whole day off work for the week led to a crisis. What it usually led to was a rested, more competent, more peaceful me. And that was a very good thing.

Now that my 'work' consists of two days of paid work and the rest of the time trying to get my own business off the ground I think I might find it a little harder to take a break. Harder to trust that it will all be OK. But I want to all the same. Because I want to remember that it's not all about me, about my business. I don't want to disappear into the rabbit hole of entrepreneur burnout.

So what does a Sabbath, a weekly day off, look like?

I don't believe that a Sabbath needs to always be taken on a Sunday. I don't think that we need to spend the day sitting quietly and reading religious texts. I love the idea of preparing meals and such beforehand and not doing any work at all, but I don't think that is achievable for most of us, and for some of us doing housework and cooking is a way to relax – a different way of being than we have for the rest of the week at work.

When Moz and I were doing missions training (back in the day, before we were married) we took Sundays off. We would go to an early church service and then we would just spend time together, chatting, maybe exploring the neighbourhood. We didn't even have to cook meals because we were living in a missions community. It was a true day off.

Now life looks different for us. Yesterday, for me the day off meant that I did a whole lot of washing, and went grocery shopping, and spent a few hours in the kitchen cooking up a proper meal for my family. I tried out a couple of new recipes and I enjoyed the creativity. I read a book. And I topped the day off by watching a mindless chick-flick.

Eugene Peterson describes his Sabbath in his book *The Pastor*.[22] When he was a pastor, he would take a day off each Monday, and he wrote to his congregation to explain what he was doing and why. He and his wife would pack a lunch and go for a bush walk each Monday (or a hike I guess, he was in America, here in Australia we would call it a bush walk). For the morning they would walk in silence, just taking the time to process the week that had come before. But when they broke for lunch they would talk to each other and they would keep talking all the way home.

Kristine Rusch just happened to talk about her weekly day off in her blog the week I was writing this.[12] She writes that she takes the day off from work and that she has a no screen rule with that day off. 'No email, no iPad, no laptop,' she writes, 'phone with me but set on do not disturb except for the handful of people who call in for an emergency.' She also writes, by the way, that once she started doing this resting, her productivity increased because her stress levels went down.

Perhaps if you are parents of small children your day off would include meeting another family at a park for a play – or possibly taking your kids to one of those indoor play centres so that you can sit and read with a nice coffee. Perhaps it means using disposable nappies for one day a week so that you can take one day off the washing.

There are many options and it's not a one-size-fits-all deal. But however you put it together, I encourage you to take time off somehow to rest and rejuvenate each week.

How do you take a day off? What would your perfect Sabbath look like?

CHAPTER FIFTEEN

How to help others say no

I've talked in this book about organising time, about figuring out priorities, about making rules beforehand so that we don't have to make *yes*-or-*no* decisions on the fly, about pushing ourselves sometimes, and resting regularly. I want to finish with something that came up the other day when I was chatting to some good friends over lunch.

We were talking about the blog and the conversation moved to discussing methods of asking people to do things in such a way that they feel free to say *no*. It got me thinking about things from the other side of the fence and I thought I'd explore the idea.

An interesting thing changed for me as I've written the blog series. People started to change the way they were asking me to do things. They would preface the request with 'you can say *no*, but …'

You can say *no*, but would you like to come to the quiz night on Saturday?

Feel free to say *no*, but would you like to be a part of this fundraiser?

I know you'll probably say *no*, but there's a dinner on and I'd love you to come.

It's been wonderful. My friends are so great. They can see that I'm working on something here and they are trying to help.

Some requests are not so easy to refuse.

I think one of the worst ways of being asked is this, 'What are you doing on March the 21st?'

This method of asking assumes that if there is nothing booked into your calendar then you are available for whatever event the person is asking you to.

However, what if there is nothing booked in your calendar because you need the day off as a rest day? Or sometimes you even need to wait and see – if the week before turns out to be huge, then maybe you need to turn the event down.

Now this is difficult, because sometimes the person asking really needs to know how many people are attending an event so that they can plan properly. And sometimes people are putting off answering because they are waiting to see if a better offer arrives, and that's, honestly, a little rude.

Tasmanians have a dreadful habit of booking tickets to things at the very last moment. We've had some big name performers cancel their tours because people couldn't make up their minds whether or not they wanted to come. I guess this is another place where there needs to be a bit of balance.

Having said that, I still think there's a better way of asking.

How about, 'Hey, could you check your calendar and get back to me? I'd love to invite you to this thing on March 21st if you would like to come. I need to know numbers by the 20th of February.'

Or, 'I'd really like to get together with you for dinner, I know you're busy but I'm free on these days. Would you be able to make it on any of those? Or maybe you could suggest one that works for you? I don't mind how long I have to wait, I'd just like to spend time with you.'

Or, 'There's this really great event happening that I'm sure you'd like. Have a think about it and get back to me.'

I can see a pattern in these invitations, they all give the invited person time to think. This may purely be my introverted nature, but I really hate being put on the spot. I like to have a chance to think about anything before I give an answer. So maybe this is what we can do. Give our friends time to think and the freedom to say *no* without guilt.

DECEMBER

So here I am, writing this at the very end of December 2017, wondering what the new year will bring.

I read a book about starting your own business last week as I lay on the couch ailing with the flu and wishing that my energy levels would return. (They have today.) It said that one mistake people make when starting their own business is that they think they will have more time. That people start running their own business so that it will give them more time. They said it won't. That you will have less time, not more, running your own business.

Ouch.

I mentioned it to Moz, feeling quite concerned. I mean, what have I made all these changes for if nothing will actually get better? But he brought his wisdom to the situation.

He said, 'More time for what?'

That's the point, really, isn't it? We all have the same amount of time. We all have the same 24 hours in a day, 168 hours in a week. The question is, what do you want to do with it?

What do I want more time to do? I want more time to write, more time to read. So I am starting a business that will require me to spend more time writing and more time reading. It will look like I'm working but I'll be doing what I want to do.

I want more energy to be able to use the time I have, and I think that the changes I have made will give me more energy as I work more by myself and give out less to students. I hope so, anyway.

I am not stupid enough to think that I have now cleared the clouds and that my life will be easy from here on. I don't even think my life will be simple from here on. There will be difficult decisions to make, there will be priorities to define, there will be times when

I'm exhausted, and times when I'm full of energy. And that's just me. I will also need to take into account Moz's needs, my parents' needs, my friends, my children. I don't live in a vacuum. And I'm really glad I don't.

But I hope that as I put into practice what I have learned in this Year of Saying No *I will be able to fulfil more of the purpose I was put on this earth to fulfil. And that, my friends, is exciting.*

Thank you so much for joining me on this journey. I pray that each of us grows in wisdom about when to say no *and when to say* yes *so that our lives fill up with meaning, joy, and peace.*

I hope that you also will find and continue to move into fulfilling your potential.

Here's to saying NO.

You can find me online and sign up to my writer newsletter at www.ruthamos.com.au or you can find the blog at https://aquietlife-blog.wordpress.org. I look forward to hearing from you.

Sources

1. aquietlifeblog.wordpress.com
2. For more information see www.16personalities.com/personality-types
3. Glei, Unsubscribe: How to Kill Email Anxiety, 2016, PublicAffairs, New York City
4. www.youtube.com/watch?v=SqGRnlXplx0
5. DeSalvo, The Art of Slow Writing, 2014, St Martin's Press, New York City
6. TerKeurst, The Best Yes, 2014, Thomas Nelson, Nashville Tennessee
7. Acuff, Quitter, 2015, Ramsey Press, Brentwood
8. Hebrews 12:1
9. James 1:6
10. Galatians 6:5
11. Ephesians 2:10
12. kriswrites.com
13. www.treasuringmothers.com
14. Guinness, The Call, 2003, Thomas Nelson, Nashville Tennessee, p165-166, & 169
15. Hunt, The Complete Cheapskate, 2003, St Martin's Griffin, New York City
16. Romans 8:1
17. www.daysforgirls.org
18. www.thecreativepenn.com/careerchange/
19. www.deanwesleysmith.com
20. australia.alpha.org
21. www.jo-anneberthelsen.com
22. Peterson, The Pastor, 2012, HarperOne, San Francisco
23. Swenson, Margin: Restoring Emotional, Physical, Financial, and Time Reserves to Overloaded Lives, 2004, NavPress, Colorado Springs
24. TerKeurst, The Best Yes, 2014, Thomas Nelson, Nashville, p133-135
25. organizingpro.com
26. www.razoo.com/organization/Christian-Performing-Artists-Fellowship-2
27. rsc.anu.edu.au/~mcoote/
28. Deuteronomy 6:10-12

29. In Rusch, The Freelancer's Survival Guide, 2013, WMG Publishing, Lincoln City
30. www.calvin.tas.edu.au/oliebollen-festival/
31. Milne, Winnie-the-Pooh, 1926, Methuen Children's Books, London

www.ingramcontent.com/pod-product-compliance
Lightning Source LLC
Chambersburg PA
CBHW051952290426
44110CB00015B/2216